INFLUENCE UNLEASHED

Forging a Lasting Legacy Through
Personal Branding

VICTORIA PELLETIER

Influence Unleashed: Forging a Lasting Legacy
Through Personal Branding
Copyright © 2024 by Victoria Pelletier. All rights reserved.
Published by Unstoppable You LLC
www.victoria-pelletier.com
Cover design by 100 Covers
Print edition ISBN: 979-8-9896797-0-6
Ebook edition ISBN: 979-8-9896797-1-3
Audiobook edition ISBN: 979-8-9896797-2-0
Printed in the United States of America on acid-free paper.
Library of Congress Cataloging-in-Publication Data on file.

CONTENTS

Preface: An Unusual Story of Personal Branding.................. i

Introduction: Elevate and Accelerate: Personal Brand as the Catalyst for Your Career Advancement vii

Part I: Character Development 1
  Chapter 1: Defining Personal Branding 3
  Chapter 2: The Three Acts of Engagement.................... 13

Part II: Key Elements of Building Your Brand Story..... 29
  Chapter 3: Developing Your *Why*................................ 31
  Chapter 4: The Arena of Identity 47

Part III: A Foundation of Distinction 59
  Chapter 5: What You "Do"—Subject Matter Expertise and Thought Leadership 61
  Chapter 6: What Makes You, YOU? 71

Part IV: Longevity and Legacy of Your Brand 75
  Chapter 7: Building a Brand of Distinction: Your Unique Value Proposition.................................. 77
  Chapter 8: Legacy and Impact 87

Part V: Putting It All Together 103
  Chapter 9: Putting Your Brand into Action................ 105
  Chapter 10: Measuring Your Brand Impact................ 119

Summary.. 127
Acknowledgements.. 133
About the Author 135

PREFACE:

AN UNUSUAL STORY OF PERSONAL BRANDING

I live in Miami Beach, Florida. During a stretch of late summer, I join my neighbours in watching the weather forecast for the tropical storms that threaten the land from the sea. If a tropical beach is your home, you know precisely what I'm talking about.

During hurricane season a few years ago, I read a story about a cow residing in Charleston, South Carolina. This cow doesn't live on a farm; instead, the cow perches atop a pedestal overlooking one of the major thoroughfares through the city. Bessie, the "Coburg Cow," is a fibreglass specimen who has "watched" over Highway 17 for generations. Her location is on Google Maps, and she even has Yelp Reviews. She fares well with 4.9 stars from the 18 reviews she's been given. Scotty C. from North Charleston writes in his Yelp review, "Who doesn't love a magical cow dancing in the sky above the gridlocked traffic below. Not only does this cow statue spin, she also gets a makeover for the holidays. It's also a good indicator that an approaching storm is worth storming the grocery store for milk and bread because if things are looking glum, they take her down for safekeeping . . . or maybe for the safety of the passengers below."

Bessie is quite the superstar, and she's only a statue. If you think this whole personal brand thing isn't for you, consider the power of Bessie, an inanimate object with a personality, a story, and value she creates for the community. If Bessie can do it, you certainly can. Sure, Bessie doesn't have a brain or a heart, so she doesn't feel fear or worry about what others might think of her, but she is a symbol of resilience and longevity.

Bessie was placed on a ten-foot high platform on the Savannah Highway in 1959. At the time, this was the entrance to the former Coburg Dairy Farm, which had evolved into a distributor of dairy products in the South. Over the last 63 years, Bessie has weathered the many storms and elements that have battered Charleston Country, including winds that exceed 58 miles per hour, hundreds of flood and hail events, and 48 tornadoes.

Kind of reminds me of building my own personal brand! There have been more than a few rough patches. But my aim in this book isn't to intimidate you with tales of branding woes. Instead, I want to ignite excitement and enthusiasm within you for the thrilling possibility of bravely stepping into the spotlight and embracing your authenticity and vulnerability as a way to build your own distinctive brand. In a world yearning for genuine communication, this is crucial. We find ourselves in the midst of a loneliness epidemic and a downward emotional spiral. The way to counter this is by offering the world our authentic, dynamic human selves.

Whenever a hurricane heads toward Charleston, affectionately known as the "Holy City," locals often gauge the impending storm's severity by observing Bessie, and not just relying on the Weather Channel's predictions. Bessie's unique symbolism adds a touch of entertainment and simplicity to the otherwise daunting storm preparations. Again, there's a parallel to my journey in shaping my personal brand as a leader. In times of turmoil, whether it's a pandemic, economic challenges, or social upheaval, people have consistently turned to me for guidance, insight, and support. My real-world experiences and the wisdom I bring to the table have made my voice a sought-after beacon during these stormy periods. And it is this—being in a position to help others—that brings me my greatest satisfaction.

Why do I care about a cow statue parked on a road 600 miles from my home? It's not just because her journey is a bit like mine. And no, please don't crack any cow jokes or start calling me Bessie! It's because Bessie started out as a mascot for a company, much like I became known as an expert within, and then the face of, many of the companies I have worked for. Now, Bessie is known by virtually everyone in the Southeast as a beacon of safety when a big storm hits.

Like Bessie, who has now given "birth" to a calf which stands beside her, I'm still evolving. My personal brand continues to develop. If you talk to me in ten years, I will tell you the same. When I look back, though, I can appreciate how far I have come. Far enough to have an audience big enough to write this book. Far enough to have collected plenty of stories of stumbling, feeling frustrated, and breaking through to the other side of the tough parts. That's pretty cool, but what's even better are the times that people tell me I helped them through the storm.

In Charleston, after the storm clears, the dairy cleverly capitalizes on the situation with advertisements that showcase

Bessie, assuring everyone of her well-being. These ads blend a touch of whimsy and humour, highlighting the cow's unique role as a makeshift weather barometer. As a result, people aren't just reaching for any milk; they're specifically seeking Bessie's. This exemplifies the essence of personal branding. It transcends job titles, company affiliations, and skill sets by leveraging the power of storytelling. As a living, breathing human—not a statue of a cow—the authenticity of your narratives, drawn from your own experiences, directly influence how much you resonate with and engage your audience.

Twenty-plus years ago, I didn't have the term "personal brand" in my professional vocabulary. I knew I was a leader, and others had told me that I was very talented at most tasks put in front of me. Over time, I was able to narrow in on those particular strengths that were backed by passion. Unbeknownst to me, this is how I began the process of uncovering what I would later define as my unique value proposition, a key element in the brand-building process. Little did I know that it would not only help my audience, but would help me grow professionally and personally.

I knew my unique value proposition stemmed from my moving backstory. I had a difficult past. From the chaos of being reared by a mixed-up, dysfunctional addict to the loss of my ex-wife many years later, overcoming my biggest challenges and coming out the other side as a new, stronger, more compassionate person became the core of my brand— the signature mark I became known for.

I wrote *Influence Unleashed* to help you make an impression on the world by developing your own, unique personal brand identity, regardless of your background. Your journey might echo a classic "rags to riches" tale, a transformative "breakdown to breakthrough" narrative. Or perhaps it's intertwined with certain privileges you've encountered. As you delve into this book, remember Teddy Roosevelt's wise words: "Comparison is the thief of joy." Instead of drawing comparisons, I encourage you to find inspiration in my story and the examples shared in this book. This is an opportunity for genuine enjoyment, a rare moment for you as a leader to focus entirely on yourself. You might be thinking, "Isn't the whole point of a personal brand to attract an audience?" True, but your unique allure will naturally emerge when you prioritize understanding, embracing, and communicating your own story first. If you can accomplish this, you will not only ensure you connect with the right audience—the right audience will strive to connect with you.

A brand is essentially an amalgam of perceptions held by your audience, shaped by your story and experiences, and reflective of your reputation. It resides at the confluence of your narrative and how your audience perceives it. Success in branding hinges on clearly articulating and comprehending this narrative. When I embrace my brand, I'm not just presenting myself: I'm showcasing the best version of who I am, a version that has evolved and refined over time. As you engage with this book, if you stay committed and fully immerse yourself in its teachings, you'll gain a deep understanding of what constitutes the core of *your* personal brand.

INTRODUCTION:

ELEVATE AND ACCELERATE: PERSONAL BRAND AS THE CATALYST FOR YOUR CAREER ADVANCEMENT

Who am I? What do I do? These are two important questions I have had to ask myself many times as my personal brand-building journey evolved. What about you? Are you stuck trying to figure out how to show your whole self publicly without feeling like you have a constant vulnerability hangover? Do you often question if there is enough value in you to garner the audience you are looking to engage? Have you found yourself comparing the way you show up with others who may be experiencing more success than you? Is the advice you have so far received about this daunting, overwhelming, and prescriptive? Rest assured, you are among many professionals looking for guidance when it comes to building a personal brand that feels like you and that helps you find new levels of personal and professional success and satisfaction.

Would *you* follow you? The answer to that question might be yes or no right now, but the goal by the time you get to the end of this book is that the answer is yes—and not just yes, but *hell yes*. While I always say there's nothing linear about personal brand building, you deserve a framework. All of those times I threw spaghetti at the wall to see if it stuck, I kept thinking how great it would be to have a guide to help me be more surefooted.

Today, I realize I likely wouldn't be able to be a great coach for you if I hadn't served my time in the trenches. So, here we are, in it together, and I am going to lead you through the Influence Unleashed method step by step until we reach the top together. And because I am a fitness fanatic, I would like to remind you that it's always good to keep training on the same staircase. After our first flight together, I invite you to strengthen those leg muscles and come back for more.

Owning your professional identity in the digital world is becoming increasingly important. The fact is, the internet is most likely the first place people will go to learn about who you are. While personal branding isn't solely built on the internet, it is likely where those who you have yet to meet in person will go to find out about you before they engage with you. On the flipside, after your audience hears your keynote speech, it is likely they'll do an online search to learn more about who you are, increasing their engagement with you. Online access can expand in-person opportunities and in-person events, and private work can be validated and reinforced through your digital persona. Helping you unify the two through the building of an effective personal brand that unleashes your influence, so that you can achieve the outcomes you desire, is the purpose of this book.

Because I dramatically increased my personal and professional opportunities when I took agency over my identity, I embarked on a journey to help others do the same. If you have even just a LinkedIn profile, you are already exposing yourself, prone to outside assessment and judgement that will be based on your public image. No matter how few followers you currently may have, you do have an online presence.

Utilizing the Influence Unleashed method I have developed, I have been able to educate and coach thousands of people to develop their personal brand and be able to clearly articulate their identity and uniqueness. Personal branding goes far beyond a resume and LinkedIn profile page that tell only your professional story; instead, it allows your whole self to shine by sharing your professional *and* personal lived experiences. Throughout this book, I will share with you the building blocks of creating a personal brand that will help you stand out, establish credibility and trust, expand visibility and accessibility, build meaningful, long-term relationships, and achieve personal and professional aspirations.

My Personal Branding Journey

Before I helped others unleash their influence, I had to help myself do the same. This book is based on my own trials and triumphs that helped me learn and grow my personal brand into something that represents what is authentically me in every context of my life.

Two decades ago, I was told by a colleague that I had earned the moniker "The Iron Maiden" at work. While I wasn't offended at first, believing the nickname was complimentary of my strength in maintaining an attitude that was strictly business, it did not represent who I was at my core. Eventually, I made the decision to show more empathy at work, displaying a side of me that was well-known in my personal life but entirely left behind when I entered the work hours of the day. Today I am recognized for a leadership style centred on humanity and empathy, and on my unwavering commitment to diversity, equity, inclusion, and the advancement of women and the LGBTQ+ community. I've also gained recognition for nurturing leaders and fostering robust corporate cultures. That's the difference personal branding has made in my life.

"The Iron Maiden" didn't even come close to describing who I was as a whole human. Back then, I was suffocating valuable parts of my life and character. I would later use heart-centred leadership to drive impact. From helping large corporations deliver profit through purpose, to coaching leaders on how to increase employee engagement, the more I took agency over my brand, the bigger impact I would make.

I had been given the nickname based upon others' perceptions, and because I had been withholding certain facets of my authentic self. While I garnered respect in the workplace, I suspect that more people may have feared me rather than been inspired to follow me. The team could rely on my unwavering focus on business and on my providing a sense of predictability, but my true personality remained absent from the arena.

During my tenure at several of the large corporations I have worked for, I have seen many of my colleagues showing up online, exclusively, as their job title at our company or as the subject matter expert in their field. By focusing exclusively on their expertise or specialty in their messaging, or by sharing only company marketing collateral on their social media profiles, they offered no hint as to who they really are— let alone why they're different from all of our competitors. Presenting themselves in this way looked like a never-ending sales pitch, and I pictured thousands of people scrolling right past their posts, because plainly and simply, there was absolutely no human connection to be made.

My professional career has spanned 30 years at this point; however, it wasn't until maybe 15 or 20 years ago, when I learned to be more empathetic and vulnerable at work, that I understood the power of human connection that stems from sharing our lived experiences as leaders and influential people. Back then, I was a version of these one-dimensional colleagues of mine. Maybe you are experiencing this yourself. When I began sharing my story, I realized that there were millions of experts but there was only one *me*. It's the perfect time to begin your personal brand building journey; there's only one *you*, and you have a unique advantage when you appeal to humanity through learning how to be yourself authentically and confidently.

When I stepped into my first executive leadership role, I was a 24-year-old COO who had been given what was a stretch role for me, but one based on my strong work performance and extreme work ethic. Because I had achieved so much at a young age through the method of outwardly near-emotionless leadership, the rewards I was reaping encouraged my behaviour until I realized that no one at work saw the softer sides of me—the sides that were about how I created value in my personal relationships. Through embracing empathetic leadership I shifted how I led and built stronger relationships. And I began building my personal brand, leading me to share personal stories with the goal of empowering others to move through adversity with an #unstoppable life philosophy, a #noexcuses mindset, and a #radicalcandor approach.

My Purpose for Writing this Book

I wrote this book because helping people come forward authentically through personal branding brings me joy. As you've just read, I've been there myself! I've experienced the downside of not having an intentional personal brand, and now I enjoy the very rewarding upside of having a brand that truly reflects my authentic self. Yes, I have garnered various credentials and awards that point to my role as a leader in the world of personal branding, but it's my personal life experience that is the true foundation for the material in this book. One of my favourite quotes by George Addair is, "Everything you've ever wanted lives on the other side of fear." This is most certainly what personal branding has taught me, and it's why I so urgently want to share with you the branding framework presented in this book. My goal is simple: I want to give people the courage to be themselves, particularly when it comes to leadership—and we are *all* leaders, regardless of titles or hierarchy.

By helping you unleash your influence, together we can create a contagion of courageous and positive leadership. We can be examples for others. We can communicate to them the power of showing up in person.

Some years ago, I was hired by a company to lead a troubled client portfolio. My first challenge was simply to find a way onto the calendar of one of the top client executives so we could hold a crucial kick-off meeting. It was only through a chance encounter at a hockey arena where both our children were playing that our relationship began. We bonded over being "hockey moms," and this personal connection was the thing that changed our dynamic and forged a productive partnership. This important relationship was a key factor in making progress in my role and delivering results. Human connection happens when we show that we are whole people, whether we are live and in-person or online.

How the Influence Unleashed Method Works

The Influence Unleashed method empowers you with the ability to take charge of your brand. Mastering your personal brand allows you to shape perceptions and guide how others see and understand you, ensuring your narrative is fully represented rather than leaving it to chance without your direct guidance.

As you weave your expertise and actions with your personal stories and identity, you increase your credibility and deepen the trust with your audience. Bolstered by the full and authentic presentation of yourself that you have molded, the insights you impart become not only informative and rich in content but also more influential, simply because they're coming from *you*. Revealing your personal facets invites your audience to connect and engage with you on a deeper level, fostering a lasting relationship as they come to truly know you.

As you build out your personal brand identity, you'll notice your network will expand, seemingly of its own accord. You'll find yourself pleasantly surprised by the burgeoning web of connections you cultivate, including the strengthening bonds within your existing network and the fresh ties with new clients and influencers.

And here's the big payoff: As your identity becomes familiar and your trustworthiness well-established, reaching your goals becomes significantly more attainable. Why? Because people will *want* to help you achieve them. They know and understand you as a real person, a friend and ally, and they will come to see your success as being a part of their own.

Unleashing your influence isn't a haphazard journey; it requires a structured approach. This book guides you through the entire personal branding journey, beginning with the crucial first step of character development. Everyone deserves a reliable guide on this path, and I pledge to be that partner for you. Together, we'll demystify what personal branding really means and how it's distinct from being defined as a subject matter expert or a thought leader. We'll also examine the interplay between these three elements.

Embarking on this journey requires courage, so I'll introduce you to the Three Acts of Engagement, which are foundational behaviours in personal brand building designed to endure the tests of time. To undertake this work effectively, you need a clear purpose, an understanding of why your personal brand is important to you. This will enable you to project your brand authentically from the inside out. By building a strong, differentiated brand, you ensure that your audience sees the real you, granting you the freedom to present yourself and stand out in a manner that truly reflects your identity, beliefs, and values.

The essence of shaping your personal brand's character boils down to understanding and embracing the mindset from which you operate. This critical aspect is what we will pinpoint and harness in the initial part of this book.

In the book's second part, you will build your personal brand focusing on four key foundational areas. We will start with where most people stop, the fundamental element that I believe is the easiest component of personal brand building: leveraging your expertise. Learning to seamlessly incorporate your existing education, knowledge, and subject matter expertise into your personal brand is key to establishing your credibility.

Next, we'll dive into how identifying and showcasing your passions plays a crucial role in shaping how you present yourself. I will guide you in recognizing both personal and professional passions, layering them onto your existing expertise. This approach ensures your brand is enriched with stories and wisdom drawn from your own life experiences.

Developing a personal brand that helps you stand out is both highly rewarding and the most challenging aspect. Your task is to craft a unique and differentiated brand. Once you successfully differentiate yourself, people are more willing to invest a premium to collaborate with you.

The last foundational element of personal brand building will be the crucial shaping of your legacy, meaning the impact you've made for which you want to be known for. By setting clear goals based on what you aim to be recognized for, you lay a solid foundation that shapes and guides the evolution of your personal brand's mission and strategy over time.

Investing your time in this process is worthwhile only if you recognize that effective personal branding is built to last. In the concluding section of this book, we'll bring everything together, enabling you to confidently apply what you've learned so you can unleash the impact you aspire to make in the world.

You might not yet realize the immense power of who you are and the significance your life experiences hold in the world. Take, for example, Coburg Dairy's decision to place Bessie the cow above the highway. It's unlikely they anticipated her becoming such a treasured part of the community. Similarly, within you lies a unique value, a personal "weather vane" that you might not have discovered yet. When Bessie was first removed, it was just to protect her from an approaching storm. But that simple act unexpectedly amplified her influence because people in the area had learned to look for her. Now, it's your turn to unlock and showcase your own influence.

PART I:

CHARACTER DEVELOPMENT

CHAPTER 1:

DEFINING PERSONAL BRANDING

"To become more fascinating, you don't have to change who you are. You have to become more of who you are."
—Sally Hogshead, Fascinate: How to Make Your Brand Impossible to Resist

"The demise of my self-worth didn't arrive through a single, catastrophic event. No, the dissent was gradual. Insidious. One cut at a time." This quote is the opening line in a video I recorded and posted to YouTube several years ago entitled "Death by a Million Cuts—A Journey to Self-Love." I recorded this when I was a senior executive at IBM, and continuing to build my personal brand. This vulnerable (for a speaking event) talk is one of many recorded moments in which I have openly related my personal story to develop trust by sharing a sensitive side of myself. Doing this talk, and others like it, connected me with a network of people who would resonate with the messaging I wanted to bring to the corporate world and beyond. This evolved into the brand identity I have today.

The 21st-century personal branding movement has evolved, and social media channels are packed with millions of influencers. So, how do *you* stand out from the rest? Like me, the way forward is to reach deep inside yourself and answer the question, Who am I? For most people, the answer will be formulating a combination of your subject matter expertise and your lived experiences that will help you stand out, elevate your presence, and differentiate your brand. That's why it's called *personal* branding; it's the process of defining your identity through expressing who you are.

Leveraging your area of expertise—what you *do*—is often the easiest part of establishing your personal brand because more than likely it's something you are already intimately familiar with. You probably have an idea of how what you do creates value for others. It's worth mentioning here that chapter 5 covers the *what you do* part of the process in detail, and includes specific information for people with subject matter expertise and thought leadership backgrounds. Your background is an important part of personal branding that establishes *credibility* to back up your brand.

But when it comes to the *who you are* part of the formula, things get more challenging because you're dealing with your vulnerabilities. Examining the valuable, identity-forming lived experiences that you want to share is core to personal branding. Personal branding, as differentiated from merely communicating *what you do*, creates connections that establish trust with your audience. By sharing elements of your personality and lived experiences that define the narrative arc of your life, you set yourself apart. It's all about being true to yourself, walking the talk, and ensuring your beliefs and values align seamlessly with your words and actions across every facet of your life.

Building a personal brand involves some serious work, including developing a robust professional network that, when built effectively, results in helping you actualize your primary goal, be it landing your dream job, speaking on stage, getting a book deal, or becoming a brand ambassador.

Personal Branding: Defining Who You Are

Corporations have fostered employee personal branding since *Fast Company* introduced the concept in 2005. Today, however, many corporations have come to view employee personal branding as a strategic imperative, given the fall of corporate brand ad campaigns and the rise and power of thought leaders and influencers and "social selling." This is something you can use to your advantage.

In a 1997 essay titled *The Brand Called You,* management expert Tom Peters defined the core precept of personal branding. He wrote: "You don't 'belong to' any company for life, and your chief affiliation isn't to any particular 'function.' You're not defined by your job title or confined by your job description. Starting today, you are a brand."

When done effectively, from a place of personal development and growth, your personal brand humanizes you in this digital age. If you are worried that personal branding will be a shallow exercise to create an influencer out of you, I guarantee you it is the opposite of that. Yes, you will expand your influence, but more importantly, you will have agency over your image and presence, and opportunities to impact what matters most to you. Personal branding is about depth and dimension, not surface level appearances.

With effective personal branding, you will create so much value for your audience that you will be sought out by recruiters for potential new roles. You will be given the clout you need to increase your consulting fees. You will be in demand as a keynote speaker. Or perhaps your goal is to be published in a major publication. If so, personal branding is the way to showcase who you are and what you are all about so you can capture the attention of your target audience. If there's one word to remember when it comes to remembering why personal branding is so important, it is *trust.*

Presenting yourself to the world solely through your job title, educational qualifications, industry, or company affiliation, as important as these things may be, does not constitute personal branding. In my view, such an approach is significantly lacking if it doesn't reveal who you are beyond these elements. You are much more than your job title, your resume, your field of study, your employer, or where you were educated. I've noticed a common misconception where individuals think they have established a personal brand by merely highlighting these aspects online, focusing on sharing content about their company's products, services, or strictly educational material. This is a narrow view of what personal branding truly encompasses.

It's widely accepted, and I wholeheartedly concur, that we've merely scratched the surface of the personal branding era. I firmly believe in the immense value of personal branding because it offers you the chance to humanize yourself, creating connections with others and setting you apart in the process. This is why it's crucial to base your personal branding on the essence of who you authentically are. By following the steps outlined in this book and adopting a mindset that recognizes the gradual, incremental successes brought by personal branding, you will achieve your goals, provided you persist through the challenges.

Unravelling the Paradox: Personal Branding's Chicken-and-Egg Dilemma

My leadership journey inside the companies I have worked for has been compelling and my pathway unique, like yours will be, depending on where you are in the process. You might be wondering where you should start. In personal branding, there are various pathways that you can take. Does being a subject matter expert, as an example, lead to building a personal brand? Or does your personal brand effort qualify you to be a subject matter expert? What comes first? It's impossible for me to tell you, but the great news is that you have a choice in the matter.

My recommendation for you is that you begin with where you are most developed and strong. The personal branding path that made the most sense and was most obvious to me was to start by capitalizing on my substantial experience as a subject matter expert (SME), which led into further refining my brand through the sharing of my lived experiences, and then expanded into thought leadership.

Whether you're beginning your journey as a SME like I did, or as a thought leader akin to the various renowned public figures I'll reference throughout this book, personal branding is essential for setting yourself apart. We will explore the natures and roles of SME and thought leader, and how they relate to personal branding, throughout this book. In my experience, focusing on your personal brand as the first step is not mandatory for you to unleash your influence; rather, it is a must-do at some point on your professional development journey. This is because the roles of SME or thought leader, while invaluable for establishing expertise and credibility, don't fully capture the essence of who you are. That's where personal branding comes in, at the point where you get up the courage to express the fullness of who you are. It's your unique identity that forges connections with others and drives the spread and influence of your personal brand, ultimately determining the impact you can make.

The impact I knew I was making became evident in my time as a SME and business leader through strong performance results and outcomes and increases in employee satisfaction and engagement. Team members shared with me that I had positively impacted their personal development and overall work experience. This motivated me to share my experiences more broadly and initiate change on a grander scale as a thought leader.

But as I mentioned above, thought leaders and SMEs need to showcase more than expertise to differentiate themselves from other experts in their field. People latch on to messaging from people they like and trust. Through developing courage, vulnerability, and authenticity in my personal brand, I earned my audience's trust and vastly increased my stature and influence. Your route may look like mine or like the other influential people referenced as you read this book. The point I want to make for you is that there is no right way to start. The only mistake you can make, if your goal is to unleash your influence, is not incorporating personal branding along the way.

From Introverted Thought Leader to Influential Personal Brand

Let's look at a good example of somebody whose personal brand development became a crucial factor in tremendously broadening his audience and followership. Scientist Andrew Huberman started out by sharing his scientific insights, primarily in health and wellness, through his podcast "Huberman Lab." Thought leadership was his starting point. He did not at that time have a developed personal brand.

Huberman has shared that he would have remained a scientist at Stanford behind the scenes had it not been for a colleague who begged him to start the podcast. So he started podcasting, and provided so much high quality knowledge and value for his audience that soon lots of people were asking each other, "Who is this guy?" Huberman is now quite famous and enjoys a fully developed personal brand. He has taken to the live stage, where he shares short personal stories with his audience, intermittently woven through the scientific information he presents. Millions have become captivated by him, as his personal brand has made intricate scientific studies attractive and digestible to the masses.

What matters isn't what comes first. What matters is that you understand that personal branding works by understanding who you are. This is fundamental if your goal is to create impact and leave a legacy behind. I implore you to begin this process of self-exploration now, because it does take time and practice to find traction.

By way of example, when I began to focus on building my personal brand, I initially worked to set myself and my team apart in the competitive B2B professional services arena by increasing our presence at conferences and various speaking engagements. My role as a SME was centred around representing the companies I worked with, sharing expertise in business process outsourcing and contact centre operations. However, as I navigated through various segments of the professional services industry, my personal brand evolved, enriched by the extensive and varied experiences I accumulated. This took time, but the journey bolstered my confidence to open up about my lived experiences, beyond the professional arena. I started to share stories about my childhood and the values that are important to me. This shift in focus led to increased engagement on platforms like LinkedIn, and I found myself communicating a message that transcended the confines of the company I was associated with.

Developing my personal brand not only benefited the companies I worked for, but also started to positively impact individuals I had never met. Embracing authenticity in my personal branding allowed me to stand out in a crowded digital world of experts, and foster meaningful connections with my network and audience.

Personal branding revolves around *you*, and that's precisely why I've penned this book. The purpose of the Influence Unleashed method is to guide you on the journey of crafting or enhancing your personal brand. Embracing this process involves defining your authentic self, uncovering what sets you apart, exploring the convergence of your talents, passions, and purpose, and understanding how these facets contribute value to the network you aim to build and grow.

The good news is that building a personal brand is not related to how many Instagram followers you have, for example. The work we are doing together here is about the *results* that come from your followership. For somebody to like your content is one thing; for them to actually engage with and to invest in you is another. A powerful personal brand gets you the traction you need to share your stories with the world on an ever-increasing scale over time.

Delivering value consistently with authenticity and vulnerability is the foundation for building a brand that lasts. With all of the work that goes into personal brand building, making sure that you are meeting critical modern-day personal brand-building standards will help ensure that the hard work you put into the process will stand the test of time.

As mentioned, personal branding, at its core, is formed through a mixture of particular elements of yourself and the contexts of your life. Because I have explored these elements and found success in the process, I'm honoured to share this work with you. You will quickly experience meaningful success if you consider this an exercise in personal *and* professional development. Before you expand your audience, you will raise your awareness of the details that have formed your ability to lead, and you will attract the professional network and followership you seek. They are out there, looking for somebody like you. My intent is to coach you in the art of making yourself visible, so they can find you.

My goal in this book is to guide you in unleashing your influence through crafting or enhancing your personal brand. As you continue to expand and evolve, delving deeper into your core values, discovering your *Why* (your purpose), shaping the persona you wish to be known for, and envisioning the legacy you aim to leave behind, your personal brand will naturally flourish. This book is your toolkit for constructing that lasting legacy and gaining insight into the future, empowering you to proactively lay a strong foundation upon which you can build and thrive.

CHAPTER 2:

THE THREE ACTS OF ENGAGEMENT

I'm going to begin this chapter with a pep talk about weaving emotions into the process of building your personal brand. To put it simply: emotions are essential to the process.

If incorporating personal stories, experiences, or expressing emotions in your personal brand-building efforts makes you wince, I encourage you to embrace the notion that emotions are far from superficial or sentimental. Emotions are the connective tissue of your brand, and without them, the bits and pieces of your brand become no more than isolated components. Emotions exemplify the humanness of your nature; the way you connect on a deep level with your audience. Without them, your personal brand will not be built to last. If you come forth with knowledge or wisdom but lack personalized storytelling that elicits emotions, the odds of creating value for your audience lower significantly.

According to a 2018 Motista study, 71 percent of customers make brand recommendations driven by their emotional connection to the brand. While this study examined consumer behaviour with data from over 100 retailers, I think it is a relevant comparison to personal branding. Many such studies have been conducted on how emotional attachment drives consumer behaviour. Paging through these studies, it became clear to me that meeting this emotional need is essential in personal branding as well. Not only will you generate value for your audience, but you will gain deeper insights into the essence of your personal brand and your own identity.

This chapter explores how to get your audience to engage with you on a much more invested level. The secret is to consistently practice what I call the Three Acts of Engagement: courage, vulnerability, and authenticity. These three acts demonstrate to your audience that you are a real person, with real personality traits, who has both strengths and weaknesses—in short, somebody who is just like them. This is how you forge an emotional bond with your audience, and define your personal brand in a memorable way.

Act I: Courage

"The root of the word courage is cor—the Latin word for "heart." In one of its earliest forms, the word courage had a very different definition than it does today. Courage originally meant 'To speak one's mind by telling all one's heart.'"
—Brené Brown

"How on earth am I going to do this?" This is a question I ask myself every time I step into unknown territory. I'm a person who can "fake it until I make it" with a steely sort of confidence, but underneath my exterior strength I've been scared shitless in moments where I had to speak up, speak out, and stand up for my core values. That annunciation to the world through declaring that I live a life of no excuses fueled me to write this book and to help you boldly make your mark effectively. Because I have coached and guided so many people on this topic and have seen how easy it is for many to hit the bulls-eye, I had no excuse not to put this book into action. I know that effectively building a personal brand will release the full capacity you have to positively display the nature of your character, develop yourself into a better person, and create a contagion of courage in the process.

It's important to me that you understand that people you observe who are doing something challenging are actually confident about only one thing: they know that fear is a driving force for change, and they use it to their advantage. In this case, doing something challenging means coming forth with a personal brand built on a foundation of authenticity and vulnerability. And this requires courage. As a leader, if you haven't been courageous voluntarily, you have likely at least been forced into it unconsciously from time to time because it's an unavoidable part of leadership.

Courage is the act of moving forward, even when you are uncomfortable, unsure, or fearful. Courage will be your confidence-bolstering partner in personal brand building, and consciously demonstrating courage will become an integral part of what drives you forward as you build your personal brand. Think of this book as a material representation of the type of courageous personal brand building that will set you apart simply by showing up as your whole self. That's exactly what I did in this book, and it's what you can do in whatever efforts you make before the world. As discussed later in this chapter, authenticity aligns your actions and brand with your personality and values—and courage will make sure you stay true to yourself, no matter how much pressure you are under.

Artist Damon Davis gave a short TED talk titled "Courage Is Contagious," based on the Ferguson, Missouri, protests that erupted after the fatal shooting of Michael Brown by police officer Darren Wilson on August 10th, 2014.

Davis boldly states on the TED stage, "I found anger, there was a lot of that, but what I found more of was love. People found love for themselves and the community . . ." He goes on to talk about how he transmuted the collective anger he felt with the community into photographs of the hands of the people who were present at the protests. He was determined to capture love through his art to uplift the stories of the people represented by the media as angry and destructive. The contagion of courage is well documented throughout history, and Davis showed how it manifested in his lived experience.

Davis's TED Talk is an excellent example of moral courage. "I became a conduit for all of this courage given to me . . . I think we should be conveyors of courage in the work we do . . . we are the wall between the normal folks and the people who use their power to spread fear and hate." The Ferguson protests were front and centre on every news channel, and he truly stepped up to shine a fair and unobstructed light on the community.

Journalist Daniel Ellsberg leaked a 7,000-page top-secret document from the Pentagon exposing two decades of US government deception about its involvement in Vietnam from 1945 to 1968. When he showed up at federal court in Boston in 1971, he was asked about the real prospect of going to prison. He replied, "Wouldn't you go to prison to help end this war?" Ellsberg didn't win over the masses, but he added to the fervour that caused a cataclysmic shift in conversations and public attitudes about the Vietnam War. Even with the looming threat of prison, he encouraged people to think critically and speak out for generations to come.

For leaders, practicing moral courage is especially important. Exercising moral courage implies that one is prepared to uphold one's values, even when outside pressures function as a counterweight to those values. Moral courage means "practicing what you preach," even when no one is looking. Those who demonstrate such courage build trust with their stakeholders.

If those following or looking on know that the one providing leadership does so consistently and will not fold under pressure, they will follow. Courage is contagious. Eventually, those who experience courageous leadership in others will begin to exercise their own boldness when confronting challenging situations.

Throughout *Influence Unleashed*, I show you stories of people who demonstrated courage as they successfully built their personal brands. I hope you are inspired by them. Being motivated by others' successes will help you connect how your own insights, experiences, and values interplay with your most prominent strengths. Knowing the strong points of your personal brand creates the confidence you need to make being courageous easier and more automatic. It's a daily requirement to move beyond fear because, as I said earlier, developing your personal brand will not be a linear process. While there is no predictable, straight line to success, I am here to help you navigate the rewarding, and oftentimes challenging, twists and turns that will help you create the impact you want to make.

When President Obama used the word *audacity*, it was about hope taking everyone by surprise. That is what courage can do. In addressing the United Nations General Assembly on September 24th, 2014, he said, "We choose hope over fear. We see the future not as something out of our control, but as something we can shape for the better through concerted and collective effort." Obama's legacy is known for the Audacity of Hope.

Courage is the first act because it is the foundation you build your brand upon, and without it you cannot be authentic or vulnerable.

Act II: Vulnerability

"It's not the critic who counts. It's not the man who points out how the strong man stumbles or where the doer of deeds could have done it better. The credit belongs to the person who is actually in the arena."
—Theodore Roosevelt

The word *vulnerability* carries a weighty and fear-inducing definition as it implies a susceptibility to harm or attack. However, the dictionary omits the positive, flip side of the coin of exposing oneself. Embracing vulnerability isn't just about letting your guard down; it's a secret superpower. By getting comfortable with being uncomfortable, you're gearing up to tackle any curveballs life throws at you. This isn't about weakness—it's the complete opposite. It's about building a kind of inner muscle, a resilience that keeps you moving forward, come what may. Think of it as your resilience gym membership—the more you show up, the stronger you get.

"Simone Biles Just Became the Greatest Gymnast of All Time, but Her Broader Legacy Is a Lesson in Vulnerability, Perspective and Courage." This headline from an article by *Inc* in 2021 is one of many lauding a bold move made by Simone Biles, one of the most decorated gymnasts in history, when she announced that she would take a two-year break from gymnastics to focus on her mental health following the Tokyo Olympic Games in 2021. At the time of Biles's public announcement about her commitment to her mental health, the COVID-19 pandemic was well underway and the workforce at large was burning out and demanding more support. Her timing in revealing her personal truths couldn't have arrived at a better time. The world needed a role model to step up for the importance of mental well-being.

In a news appearance on NBC, Simone Biles talked about her mental health advocacy: "I'm so happy to be a voice for the voiceless and to put not so much of a stigma on mental health because I feel like it impacts everybody and affects everybody on a daily basis. So if I can be a barrier breaker for that then I'm going to do it." She used her hiatus for the advancement of her own mental wellness, but also for advocating for others by becoming the Chief Impact Officer of Cerebral, an online mental health platform. Her courageousness allowed her to share that she was struggling behind the scenes, exposing a part of herself that opened up the possibility to positively impact and inspire others. In her interviews, she often remarks that it was hard to be vulnerable initially, but that over time it became easier.

I frequently emphasize that knowing I can influence even a single person's life by opening up about my challenging childhood, about being a woman in executive leadership and a member of the LGBTQ+ community, motivates me to continue embracing vulnerability. It makes it easier to know that I am helping others. Like Biles, we must summon courage first; otherwise, those compelling stories and aspects of ourselves that enable people to connect with us will merely exist as dreams or ideas.

Leaning into vulnerability can have an unexpected side effect: it makes the relentless chase for perfection seem pretty pointless. As you start to open up, you'll notice the incredible impact you're having—and it's not just about what you're doing, but who's joining you on this journey. It's like you've turned into a human magnet, attracting people who value realness over flawlessness. When Simone Biles chose to prioritize her well-being in the public eye, it wasn't just about her. It sparked a wave of support and understanding from her teammates, celebrities, and renowned athletes alike. It's like dropping a stone in water: the ripples just keep spreading. From poet laureate Amanda Gorman to Olympic figure skater Alan Rippon, many prominent figures came out in support of her and shared their own stories, thus expanding mental health awareness through their vulnerability.

When considering the personal stories you want to share, it's important to understand that being vulnerable does not mean that you have to share *everything*. We do not know every waking minute of Simone Biles's struggles. Likely, she held back pieces of information that she ultimately felt best to keep private.

Vulnerability doesn't mean forfeiting your privacy, which remains a crucial aspect of our lives. The degree of exposure you choose to embrace is entirely within your control. It's essential to remember that not everything in the arena will go smoothly. If you encounter criticism or face adversity, these experiences can motivate you to persevere. Your personal brand will not resonate with everyone; it's crafted for those you intend to connect with through your message. Attempting to please everyone carries the risk of sacrificing authenticity and diminishing the integrity of your brand. Staying true to your message and purpose should always take precedence.

As we segue into authenticity in the final part of this chapter, please remember that the truth in what you choose to expose is more important than the depth and breadth. I recommend identifying the aspects of your life stories that are yearning to be expressed. Consider which stories hold the most value in your present perspective and why you believe they should be shared with your audience. Then, well, take a stab at it and share. Start small or go big, but be sure to pay attention to the connections you make in the process.

Crafting a personal brand with clear boundaries isn't just smart, it's a game-changer. It's about striking that perfect balance between sharing and privacy. After all, everyone needs a little mystery in their life, right? The power to choose what you reveal and how much—that's all in your hands. And this is crucial because it ties directly into the heart and soul of your brand, the *Why*, which we'll dive into in chapter 3. Your *Why* is all about your purpose, the driving force behind your actions and presence. Guess what? Your audience has their own *Why*, even if they haven't figured it out yet. By being open yet selective, you're not just sharing your story, you're guiding them to discover their own.

Your fan base will resonate with your *Why* because it echoes their own. When you nail this alignment, you're not just reaching people, you're resonating with them, and that's where the magic happens. This connection is the fuel for expanding your influence and value to a wider audience. On the flip side, if your personal brand misses this alignment, it's like trying to tune into a radio station that's just out of range—you won't quite hit the sweet spot with your ideal audience. But how will you know when you've got it right? It's in the unmistakable signs: invites to speak, a surge in likes and shares, and an uptick in all kinds of interactions with your audience. That's when you'll know you've connected the *Why* dots perfectly.

Take a big breath, put yourself in the arena, consistently test your vulnerability by sharing bits of yourself with the world, establish your boundaries, and expand your followership. An arena is an ample open space that serves courageous and vulnerable acts, so go ahead, picture yourself in the centre of it all. And remember that arenas have walls and seamlessly accommodate those brave enough to take to the stage.

"Biles quashes comeback doubts, appears set for third Olympic bid," read a headline from Reuters after she returned to the gymnastic floor. The arena expanded for Biles. More people were rooting for her than ever and she reached historic levels of achievement at the U.S. National Championships in August of 2023. There's no doubt that Biles's work will go down in history as one of the most famed comebacks of all time, and in the process she showed the world what she was made of by showcasing her greatest strengths through vulnerability.

There are thousands or maybe millions of great people who do what you do and are eager to offer their expertise to all takers. Many of them, however, are not willing to expose their lived experiences and thereby forge a lasting legacy through personal branding like Simone Biles. If it's a buyer's market out there, and I assure you it is and will always be, you'll eventually discover that you have to leverage vulnerability to expand the connections with your existing audience and attract more people to your messaging. Of the Three Acts of Engagement, vulnerability, in my opinion, is the one that bridges the biggest gaps that stand between you and the goals you have for your personal brand.

Act III: Authenticity

"Too many people overvalue what they are not and undervalue what they are."
—Malcolm Forbes

Building your personal brand should be about increasing your influence and also about shaping your legacy. These goals are most rewarding when they are achieved in authenticity. When you operate from a place of genuine self-expression, you enhance the significance of your personal branding message to your audience.

Authenticity is all about keeping it real, especially as your brand evolves. At the heart of the Influence Unleashed method is personal growth, and one bit of wisdom I'd like to share is that as your success grows, you must hand in hand grow your humility and approachability. Let me put it very clearly in another way: true authenticity is the polar opposite of arrogance. So, if you catch yourself getting a bit too puffed up with success, it might be time to hit the pause button and indulge in a little self-reflection. Staying grounded is part of the journey to greatness.

Chances are, if you're flipping through these pages, you've got a burning desire to leave a positive mark on the world. Sure, gaining recognition or fame might be on your radar, but it's your *Why* that's really steering the ship. In the world of personal branding, there's a spectrum: on one end, you have the arrogant brands, and on the other, the authentic ones. Then there are the monotone brands, those that play it safe and don't quite show their true colours. These, too, lack authenticity. Understanding what authenticity isn't can be just as important as knowing what it is, especially since it's a concept that can be tricky to grasp. By recognizing the inauthentic, you get a clearer picture of what it truly means to be genuine.

A monotone personal brand is like attending a concert devoid of any emotional connection. Picture the lead singer, almost statue-like, barely interacting with the crowd. The band members look like they'd rather be anywhere else, their faces blank, eyes fixed straight ahead. You're left there in your seat, wondering why you even bothered buying a ticket. It's that lack of emotional connection, that absence of energy and passion, that makes the whole experience forgettable.

Just as you value the investment of your audience's time and energy at a show, you should equally appreciate the attention they devote to your message. By engaging them with your *Why*, you empower them to discover their own *Why*, which, as mentioned earlier, will likely mirror yours while still being unique to them.

The pivotal moment in transitioning away from my "The Iron Maiden" persona came when I confided in a colleague about crying almost uncontrollably during a movie I had recently watched. My colleague was shocked to learn that I would show so much emotion publicly. In that moment, I was crushed with the realization that my coworkers perceived me as, quite possibly, devoid of emotion. That tiny spark of expressed vulnerability ended up being the catalyst for my personal transformation. It marked my initial steps toward forging authentic connections with my team and, later, an audience far beyond the workplace.

I've been honoured with awards for the courage it took to craft a personal brand that's truly me. It's almost surreal. Who knew that just being myself would bring external recognition? This authenticity became my new addiction. As I unleashed my influence, it sparked a contagious wave of bravery within me. It encouraged me to embrace vulnerability, to really figure out who I am, and to decide how transparently I wanted to present myself to the world.

If you are genuinely committed to cultivating your personal brand, it's time to face yourself in the mirror, assess who you see, and embark on a journey to amplify your strengths.

Personal brand development involves tapping into your most significant capabilities to advocate for your authentic self and convey the most genuine essence of your identity, ultimately benefiting both yourself and your audience.

Simon Sinek frames up authenticity so simply in his YouTube video titled "How Authentic Behavior Builds Trust": "The word authenticity is too loosely used . . . What authenticity means is the things you say and do, you believe . . . People will trust you when you only do and only say what you believe." Sinek has the trust of millions of viewers of his content. They adore him because of his consistency of character and the authenticity he employs in thought leadership.

The Three-Act Promise

Courage, vulnerability, and authenticity are all acts of emotion that when purposefully and intentionally activated will engage your ideal audience and likely draw in both targeted and unexpected support. These acts are crucial to the Influence Unleashed method.

When encountering the inevitable challenges of developing your personal brand, remember to revisit the Three Acts of Engagement. I can guarantee you'll find a contagious surge of courage by actively championing your bold and authentic personal brand identity. You will grasp the essence of branding and discover how to leverage it to provide value to your clients, customers, and team members, standing out amidst a sea of competitors.

My method? Courage, vulnerability, authenticity. Always.

Where do we go from here? Your purpose, of course; the *Why* of your personal brand that makes the connection between the emotional acts of engagement with who you are and what you do. From there, we continue forward through the Influence Unleashed personal brand-building method, covering identity, distinctiveness, and ultimately opening you up to thinking about and defining the legacy you will want to leave behind.

To conclude this chapter, I can't think of more fitting words than the rallying call Damon Davis delivered on the TED stage in 2014 during his "Courage Is Contagious" talk: "Y'all, the movers and the shakers . . . the thought leaders . . . what are you going to do with the gifts you've been given to break us from the fear that binds us every day?"

PART II:

KEY ELEMENTS OF BUILDING YOUR BRAND STORY

CHAPTER 3:

DEVELOPING YOUR *WHY*

"Like with anything in your career, however, building your brand isn't a one-time thing. It will take time and effort, and it requires consistent upkeep."
—Rachel Montanez

Developing the *Why* of your personal brand is never simply about cultivating buzz, garnering hits on social media, or expanding your followers on LinkedIn and Instagram. The *Why* is *always* about purpose, personal development, providing value, and how you envision leaving the world a better place than you found it. Ultimately, you pilot your course. You are absolutely in control of your personal brand. You are the CEO of Brand You.

Developing your *Why* will increase engagement and expand your network and followership. Your purpose will drive you to show up with courage, vulnerability, and authenticity, which draws in the attention of others. And pursuing the impact you want your personal brand to make on your life and the lives of others will expand your influence. How this materializes is through compelling storytelling.

A strong foundation of *Why* will actively shape and drive your personal brand. If you lack this foundation, you have effectively decided to allow your brand to be passively created, letting others formulate the message about who and what you are, what you believe, and what you stand for. Actively creating your personal brand means being strategic and intentional about how you let the world know and understand you.

When you take ownership of your personal brand, you take control of defining your legacy. Think about how social media has shifted the power of the paparazzi. With the advent of social media, celebrities can take their own photos and choose what parts of their personal stories they want to share. By doing so, they have diminished the tabloids' role in defining their brands. You are no different. Don't you want to have some influence over how audiences see you, colleagues describe you, and competitors imitate you?

Now, let's explore the specific steps you need to take in order to define the *Why* that powers your brand.

Define What You Do

Scientist Andrew Huberman, when asked what he does, simply states, "I dedicate my life to gathering, organizing, and dispersing information, and I love every piece of it." While personal branding is about who you are, it is also important to clearly and easily define what you do. Using Huberman as an example here is quite relevant because his brand development story saw him evolve from a scientist into a widely influential thought leader. And "story" is an apt word, because storytelling is an integral part of his brand. If you listen to a podcast featuring Huberman, you will hear him relate very personal stories ranging from his relationships to his past struggles with alcohol.

Acing what you do, whether you start as a thought leader like Huberman or a subject matter expert like me, should seamlessly integrate into your personal brand. The way Huberman so simply articulates what he does makes it easy for people to understand his *Why*—and if you listen to him on any platform, he is indeed consistent in gathering, organizing, and dispersing information.

But how exactly do you go about defining what you do? I suggest you start by first examining what you are known for, and then identifying the actions you take on a daily basis to support it. What is your equivalent to Andrew Huberman's statement describing what he does? Notice that he is purposeful in not being too specific ("gathering, organizing, and dispersing information"), allowing himself room to explore while being very clear on the action part of his statement. In addition, he adds passion to his statement by saying "I dedicate my life" and "I love every piece of it," so that what he does automatically becomes more engaging because it expresses emotion. Consider what you want your audience to experience you doing. Pay attention to what people come to you for. Most likely, therein lies the answer. From there, when people ask you what you do, which you might notice happens all of the time, you can start practicing how you articulate it, and go on to test and solidify your definition.

Define Who You Are

Here's how performance artist Marina Abramovic describes her famous exhibition at the *Museum of Modern Art* (MOMA), The Artist Is Present: "The performance is really about presence. You have to be in the here and now 100 percent." Abramovic sits in a chair across from an empty seat that, one by one, is occupied by guests of the museum who sit across from her in silence, connecting without spoken words by looking one another in the eyes. In an interview done by MOMA, she says, "So you can observe this as a kind of stage for experience. Or you can really enter that space and take active participation, which actively brings you much closer to the artist, and this presence, and to your own experience." Her description of her famed performance, in my assessment of it, is so similar to the process of defining who we are. You can define who you are on the surface, or you can use your lived experiences to bring your audience closer to you and closer to their own experiences.

The *cruc*ial step of defining your Why through who you are will likely not be easy, but it is worth the work. I can tell you it took me some years to figure this out for myself. Who you are has a lot to do with identity. Identity is a complex and often perplexing subject. So much so that I have written a whole chapter on it (see chapter 6). *In his 20*20 documentary In & Of Itself, storyteller and conceptual magician Derek DelGaudio attempts to help his audience answer the simple question "Who am I?" The documentary is a filming of a live theatrical production that begins with DelGaudio asking the audience to choose a card to complete the statement "I Am."

The audience, among them Marina Abramovic, rises from their seats to choose only one card to describe who they are. A mother, a joker, a lover, a researcher . . . At the end of the process, the revelation is that every individual is so much more than one single label. When it comes to personal branding, your audience wants to know what's on your "I Am" cards—as many as you are willing to share.

The performance, however, runs deeper than that through the sharing of your lived experiences. It involves the wisdom or know-how that comes from your perspective, personal identities, and history that goes beyond what you do professionally or *your formal education.* Using The Artist Is Present as an example of communicating who you are is intended to encourage you to understand that the expressions of who you are can be put forth in both concrete and abstract ways. At the core of who you are is the depth at which your courage, vulnerability, and authenticity are experienced. The point of connection that comes through your personal brand is when your audience becomes clear on who you are.

While we throw around many "I Am" statements, it is important to be strategic and intentional about how you go about defining who you are. There is a time to give your audience what they want and a time to give them what they need. They may want to understand you through a definitive statement, but what they really need is for you to show that you are a whole human, consisting of many "I Am" statements.

This bouquet of statements will form *an* authentic and captivating Why that will give depth to your brand. Start with giving them the "I Am" statements you most want to be known for, the ones you would like to define your legacy with. And keep in mind that over time, who you are will evolve. That's why it's important that your starting point be a building point.

What "Who You Are" Is Made Of

Because figuring out "Who You Are" is such an integral part of the process of defining your *Why*, let's spend some time digging deeper. You are a human with a *story*. Your story is driven by your passions, values, and lived experiences. The makeup of your brand *Why*, when backed by all of these Who Are You elements and combined with a clear articulation of What You Do, builds trust and connects humanity.

Passion is an intense feeling of enthusiasm or excitement about something. It is a deep-seated emotion that can drive people to pursue their goals with great energy and determination. Passion can be about anything, from hobbies and personal interests to work and family. When people are passionate about something, they are often willing to put in the hard work and sacrifices necessary to achieve their goals.

Core values are the fundamental beliefs that guide a person's behaviour. They are the principles that are most important to someone, and they help to shape their decisions and actions. Core values can be about anything, from honesty and integrity to compassion and social justice. When people are aligned with their core values, they feel a sense of purpose and fulfillment.

Lived experiences are the events, interactions, and relationships that make up a person's life. They are the raw material from which people construct their identities and their understanding of the world. Lived experiences can be both positive and negative, and they can have a profound impact on a person's thoughts, feelings, and behaviours.

These three "features of who you are" are interconnected. Passion can be fueled by core values, and lived experiences can shape both passion and core values.

- A person who is passionate about environmental protection might be driven by a core value of sustainability. Their lived experiences might include working in a national park or volunteering for a conservation organization.

- A person who is passionate about teaching might be driven by a core value of education and equality. Their lived experiences might include teaching in a low-income school or developing innovative educational programs.

- A person who is passionate about music might be driven by a core value of creativity and self-expression. Their lived experiences might include playing in a band or writing their own songs.

By understanding your passion, core values, and lived experiences, you can gain a deeper understanding of yourself and your place in the world. All of these fuel your *Why*, which in turn is vital to developing your personal brand. Think of all of these as guiding you in every decision you make.

Attracting an Audience Based on Both Similarities and Differences

As you might expect, sharing who you are can appeal to those like you. But an interesting result of sharing is that it can also attract people who are not like you, but who see themselves in you because you are telling stories of your life with feeling and authenticity. When you tell your stories, you are giving others a glimpse into your world and allowing them to connect with you on a personal level.

Passion, values, and lived experiences build and connect humanity based on similarities, but they also take down barriers that divide us because of our differences. Your *Why* will attract people who feel like they need someone who understands what it's like to be them. Creating a sense of belonging and understanding based on similarities is the most immediate audience you will likely attract. We feel connected to others who share our passions, values, and experiences because we can relate to their joys, sorrows, challenges, and aspirations. This shared understanding can lead to empathy, compassion, and a sense of community.

For example, if you are passionate about music, you might connect with others who share your passion. You might attend concerts together, discuss music theory, or even play music together. These shared experiences can strengthen your bond and create a sense of camaraderie.

Similarly, valuing honesty and integrity may lead you to form connections with others who uphold these same principles. The mutual understanding and respect stemming from these shared values can foster a sense of kinship, laying the groundwork for a loyal followership.

However, the most profound followership often comes from attracting those you might not anticipate, individuals who differ from you but perhaps see in you qualities they lack or aspire to embody.

Exposure to different perspectives and experiences can broaden our understanding of the world and help us to appreciate the diversity of human experience. This appreciation for difference can lead to tolerance, acceptance, and a sense of global citizenship. I suspect the moniker "CEO Whisperer" that has been bestowed upon me is not because I mirror the typical CEO in appearance or mirror their actions, behaviours, or experiences, but rather because they resonate with the fundamental values I uphold. CEOs are, almost always, extremely driven people and, if they are smart, they want people around them with skills and talents that they do not have themselves. Being called the Turnaround Queen and being known for my #radicalcandor and living an #unstoppable life of #noexcuses, appeals to the CEOs I have worked with.

My differences, in both my skill set and my attitude, have grabbed the attention of these CEOs because they could see the value I brought to their teams. My attention-grabbing personal brand made this possible. Had I remained silent, they wouldn't even have been aware of my presence, nor would they have understood how my unique abilities could effectively complement their work.

By conveying your stories with heartfelt emotion and passion, you have the opportunity to forge deeper connections with others, contributing to a world that is more equitable and empathetic.

Your Brand *Why*

"In my entire lifetime, everything that I've spent will be quite a bit less than one percent of everything I've made. The other 99 percent plus will go to others, because it has no utility to me." These are the words of Warren Buffett, an introverted public figure who still lives in the same split level house he bought for $31,500 in 1958. The quiet billionaire, who likely has little knowledge of personal brand building, surely is one of the most compelling public-facing personas anyone has ever experienced. His actions are so clearly aligned in every area of his life. While it took Buffett several decades to begin donating to charity, he has for some time been one of the most generous philanthropists in the world.

Certain things are well known about Buffett. He doesn't buy fancy things. His fascination with businesses started at a very young age. And he is a long-time student of the science of compounding wealth. But what's his *Why*? How could we know for sure? The third-richest man in the world doesn't take to social media, like many of the other influential people examined in this book, but perhaps we can understand the meaning that moved him toward such unimaginable success by his actions. Every year Buffett invites millionaires and billionaires to his home for a lesson in philanthropy. He has convinced many wealthy people to pledge the majority of their wealth to philanthropic causes.

One of Buffett's most famous quotes—"It takes 20 years to build a reputation and five minutes to ruin it. If you think about that, you'll do things differently."—is very telling of his character. And what about his *Why*? When asked how he wants to be remembered, he answered from the perspective of his personal legacy: "That's what I call the tombstone question. What do you want on the tombstone? What I jokingly say is, I want it to say 'Here lies the oldest man who ever lived,' but what I would really have it say is 'teacher.' That's what I like doing." I'll make an educated guess that the *Why* of Warren Buffett is to teach people how to make money and convince them that the money they made should be used for the greater good.

Buffett certainly commands attention when he speaks. Despite his plainspoken manner, every person in the world is engaged and intrigued by him. It is worth noting that Buffett's largest audience includes people of great global significance, but his ideal audience are those who he can directly persuade to adopt his *Why*, the rich men and women who populate his living room every year.

Buffet, while a likeable character, is a good example that leaders don't need to be dripping with charisma to move their constituents to action. However, they must have a compelling vision that others can make their own. That's what the power of a clear *Why* can create.

How I Wrote My Story

I still remember the job interview in painstaking detail. I was young, hungry, and more than a bit naïve. I prepped for the interview for weeks before meeting with the hiring manager. I knew everything about the job that I was hoping to land. I could articulate without error the corporate vision and mission, and even the business's management structure. If asked to detail the high points of the previous year's profit and loss statement, I was prepared to dazzle all listeners with my attention to detail.

My goal for the interview was to position myself as the most prepared candidate on the interview slate. None of my competitors would out-knowledge me when they sat down with the hiring manager because I knew too much to be defeated. I knew it all. Or so I thought. What I didn't recognize that morning was that all my competitors entered the office building with the same mindset and preparation. We were all hungry that day.

"Victoria, tell me your story . . . tell me why I should hire you instead of one of the many people I'll be interviewing for the position." *Oh shit . . . I didn't prep for that kind of question!* For the next five minutes, I stumbled through some hastily constructed biography detailing my credentials and experience. Eventually, the interviewer stopped me and reframed the question: "Victoria, what is your unique value proposition?" I froze, realizing I likely wouldn't be offered the job. I understood the work but didn't understand enough about myself, or at least how to articulate it. I had no *Why* to offer. I'd spent years running from my hellscape past instead of pondering how the hard years prepped me to be a warrior in the C-suite. Needless to say, I didn't get the job. And it was only with time that I came to realize how owning and sharing my story liberally would establish my distinctiveness amid a crowded field of competitors.

If you are serious about business, particularly if you want to be an entrepreneur, then you have decided to offer something distinctive to consumers. The *Why* of your personal brand is the driver of distinction. And when it comes to branding, your distinctiveness must be obvious. Why should a client choose you over one of your competitors? What makes what you offer better than the competition? What facet of your character and unique story helps you stand out? Your answers to these questions begin to shape the *Why* of your personal brand.

Your brand *Why* is never about arrogance; it's about authenticity. Many people make the mistake of positioning their personal brand on who they wish they were or on a false narrative they believe might be more attractive to their audience. This rarely works for long. Your brand *Why* should serve as a powerful motivator for expressing your authenticity. It should be something that stems from your genuine purpose for engaging with your audience. We are all a unique amalgam of our experiences, personality traits, perspectives, and history. To be clear, your brand *Why* is right under your nose. That's why you may fail to see it at first. The challenge in developing your *Why* is likely that you are more focused on what the audience wants than the purpose you have in attracting them in the first place. If you take the audience-pleasing approach, you effectively will have no real *Why*, and your brand won't be sustainable.

Let me offer this vignette about my brand *Why*, built upon all I learned since that interview that went sideways many years ago. My professional credentials do not necessarily provide me with brand separation from my competition. My experience can be outmatched by colleagues who've done what I've done for a lot longer than me.

In my case, the uniqueness of my personal brand rises from my personal story's sharp and abrasive counters. Here's what you need to know. I didn't "arrive" at the top of the leadership niche by flaunting a family pedigree, Ivy League education, or personal connections. It was my *personal* growth in the midst of many challenges that made my rise in the corporate space possible.

I was raised in an abusive home by a teenage mother who fought addiction. I experienced profound trauma as a child. I was often on the receiving end of my mother's rage. When I was finally plucked from my childhood home, not even allowed to take my teddy bear, I wasn't sure anyone would want me.

My extended biological family, even though they were aware of the abuse I endured, took no interest in raising a young child who wasn't their own. I became an afterthought to them. When you grow up in an environment devoid of love and support, you can either give up on yourself or learn to love and advocate for the person you see in the mirror. I chose the latter.

My drive to be relentless in work, love, and purpose is rooted in the resilience I developed as a young person. Nothing can stop you when you raise yourself up and learn how to scrap. Nothing.

Is this a sob story?

No. It's my story.

I honour it and never hide from it.

Further, I see no reason to hide it from my audience.

I learned at a young age that my future—by default—would be a lot healthier and happier than my childhood. When you go through such adversity, having a vision for your life that extends beyond the short-term seems especially important. I remember a rough patch in my late twenties when I was doing a lousy job balancing work, family, and self-care. Simultaneously, I was trying to ensure my first marriage survived and thrived.

At some point, I asked myself, "Victoria, is this where you want to be in five years?" That's the kind of question that will lead to a serious reappraisal of things. I decided then and there to build a future for my family and myself that would be healthier and happier than the current iteration. That's a story of resilience. A story of vision. A story of hope. I leverage all the above to craft and articulate my distinctiveness to various audiences.

I can be out-credentialed and out-experienced by others, but I will never be out-hustled or bested on resilience. My brand is all about resilience. The resilience to overcome the challenges, improvise in a crisis, and get up and fight on when knocked to the ground.

Ultimately, every personal brand is about how you got to where you are today, and where you'll be tomorrow and the next day, and who you are becoming along the way. Your *Why* never changes. Rather, it morphs over time as you put yourself out there and actively do the work.

Remember, building a strong personal brand network is not about self-promotion, but about establishing yourself as a valuable asset to others. Having a strong *Why* means that you will approach the building of a brand with intention and purpose, you will attract the right audience, advance your career, and make a significant impact in your field.

CHAPTER 4:

THE ARENA OF IDENTITY

*"You can see it for what it is, or you can
imagine what it could be."*
—Derek DelGaudio, In & Of Itself

"Victoria was recognized as one of the 100 Global Outstanding LGBTQ Executive Role Models by *Involve*, a 2023 Woman of Influence by *South Florida Business Journal*, a top 50 business leader in technology by *Insight Magazine* in 2021, and a Mentor of the Year by *Women in Communications and Technology* in 2020. HSBC Bank awarded her the Diversity and Inclusion in Innovation Award in 2019. She was IBM's number one global social seller, as ranked by LinkedIn, in 2019 and 2020. As a prolific, motivational, and inspirational speaker, Victoria has delivered keynotes discussing the importance of personal branding and its impact on professional growth . . ."

This lengthy list of my accomplishments is an introduction to one of my many guest appearances on a webinar series I've done. Admittedly, I feel a bit uncomfortable when my experience and awards are touted like this. But simultaneously, I acknowledge that sharing achievements is merely a reflection of the tangible outcomes that have materialized during my career, so it's fair to take note of them. Communicating them to others furthers the trust I create with my audience. Trust is built through consistency in who you are, what you do, and the results you produce. My audience has gravitated toward me and expanded as the work that I have done has become noteworthy.

"I am a woman, a mother, a wife, a fitness fanatic. You will find me working out in a gym, or playing ice hockey, or people watching on an outdoor patio. I'm a passionate networker, a connector of people, a champion for diversity, equity, and inclusion . . ." My keynote speech, "Unstoppable," is filled with "I Am" statements like these, and I own them proudly, honouring the many sides of myself. Personal branding becomes truly fulfilling once you come to realize that you can relish the attention you receive while at the same time remaining true to who you are. There is no conflict between the two.

The way you see yourself will define how your audience experiences you. The topic of identity could be a book of its own, so I'm just going to focus on providing you with a few key concepts that will help further lay a healthy and solid foundation for your personal brand. I believe that taking humility, accessibility, and the strengths of both extroversion and introversion into the public arena with you is vital for the long-term success of Brand You. By making these aspects part of your brand identity, you will extend your reach even further by adding additional depth to your brand.

By the way, if you are not experiencing some fear in the arena, you are not acting with courage. This is your reminder that courageousness is *doing it*, even when you might feel fear.

Placing yourself in the middle of the arena means that you have power over your identity, but it also means that everything you do is subject to the perspective of the onlooker. Over time, you will become increasingly comfortable knowing that you are not for everyone because those who align with your brand and are motivated to move with you long-term will be more than enough to create the results you desire.

Humility

"We learned about gratitude and humility—that so many people had a hand in our success, from the teachers who inspired us to the janitors who kept our school clean . . . and we were taught to value everyone's contribution and treat everyone with respect."
—Michelle Obama

In a recent interview, I was asked to identify a mentor contributing to my rise up the corporate ladder. I pondered how to respond to the interviewer's question because I couldn't identify such a person. Why? The hard reality is that I owe much of my success and growth in corporate leadership to many examples of *poor* leadership—those who I aspired to be *nothing* like and who prompted me to choose the opposite path.

That's how it works. There are a myriad of pathways to it, but ultimately your success is defined by you. You are responsible for defining it and building it. But in the end, it also belongs to all who've mentored and counselled you, who have sipped wine with you—even those who've shown you how *not* to act. For me, the term "self-made" is defined by my history of asking for help, curating the feedback, and putting the work in to implement and employ the lessons I received. As you can see, "self-made," for me at least, was anything but doing it alone. Your audience, mentors, and personal support team all contribute to your success.

And not all of your "contributors" will have glowing things to say. In the psychotherapy modality known as Internal Family Systems (IFS), mentorship does not only come from those who cheer you on. It also comes from your critics, or, as IFS calls them, your tormentors. Every pain point you experience or person who comments inappropriately on your personal branding is a learning opportunity that can further fuel your courage and your authenticity. Don't let them discourage you. Instead, use their criticism to fuel the resilience you need to evolve and build a brand that can stand the test of time.

This is where humility can play an important role, not just in your brand's growth, but in your personal development. Practicing humility is a skill, and like any other skill, it takes time to get good at it. Choosing reflective responsiveness instead of emotional reaction in the face of criticism is an example of humility being used. In this case, demonstrating humility serves the strategic goal of curbing risk. Your clients need to know you will not be prone to impulsivity when things are difficult. They must understand that what you offer them is measured, thoughtful, and tested.

Simply put, showing a lack of emotional control or balance is not a good look. Impulsive, emotional reactions hurt trust and give the appearance of someone trying to prove something over creating value. Responsiveness helps you maintain control of your personal brand and everything that's going on in the arena.

I embrace the philosophy of Radical Candor, coined by author Kim Scott, because it compels me to address people and tough situations head-on, allowing me to navigate them effectively. This aligns seamlessly with another core value of mine—living a life of no excuses. Tor*mentors* help to clarify the value of humility, and they can teach you many lessons if you ask yourself what you can learn about yourself when you feel unpleasantly surprised. The key is not to be reactive. Take some space and reflect on how to respond. Do this on *your* schedule, not theirs. Responding is thoughtful. Reaction is chaotic, and more than that, it usually isn't even an authentic reflection of who you are. It's just your nervous system being triggered into an outburst. Showing up authentically means taking the space to mindfully create your response to anything or anyone showing up as an adversary.

This is why I view humility as being foundational to your personal brand, and front and centre in the arena. Making your strengths known must at times be complemented with the honest admission that "I *don't* know." Humility means giving credit where credit is due and asking great questions of yourself and others. To be interesting is to be interested. This is humble success.

Amid the COVID crisis, I saw a profound lack of leadership from colleagues I had previously considered good leaders. Sadly, I observed much self-aggrandizement and self-protection instead of servant leadership. Arrogance in place of humility permeates the corporate world. From protectionism to toxic patriarchy, many business leaders look out for themselves and their cadre of buddies when challenging times arrive, sacrificing talented women, LGBTQ+ persons, and black and brown colleagues to keep the existing norms intact. Did you know that females account for only 10 percent of the CEO positions among Fortune 500 companies? A humble exploration of the answer to this question would extend beyond a mere yes or no answer. The ability to ask why that statistic is present in 2024 would be a humble response that could replace an otherwise ego-based reaction. Show your followership you are curious, and they will wonder what you will do, say, and show them next.

Kevin Smith of Mighty Roar, an agency focused on digital marketing and branding, offers this vignette about the importance of humility in brand work: "Humility in marketing doesn't mean that you bow to your competition or market your brand in a self-deprecating way. It simply means you're upfront about what you offer, stand for, and your relationship with your customers." Credibility, results, and recognition are not in conflict with humility. Go forward with your accolades while simultaneously acting from your brand *Why*. Employ the Three Acts of Engagement and allow your audience the opportunity to watch you in the arena so they feel compelled to join you and help you create the impact you want to make in the world. Brand longevity happens when you maintain an ongoing, value-providing connection with your followership.

A 2020 study of CEOs by the University of Paris found that "female CEOs illustrated greater empathy, adaptability, and diversity more frequently than their male peers." A similar study by Catalyst showed that "Empathetic leaders have more innovative and productive teams and are likely to retain talent." Females in leadership demonstrate more empathy; empathetic leaders are likely to retain talent. As a women's advocate, using this data is relevant to my personal brand, but there is nothing exclusive about empathy. Men have a tremendous opportunity to infuse empathy into their personal brand, too. The heart is about looking through varied lenses and imagining the lived experiences of others through your own. There is no gender attached to being empathetic. I'm simply fulfilling the expectation of my personal brand by creating awareness of the female experience in leadership.

In your brand development, converse with your current and potential clients. Reach out to them and come to understand how their personal stories impact their vision and their decision-making. If the client offers permission, share some of these personal and powerful vignettes on your brand platforms.

One of my clients has a "Letters from Home" feature on her personal website. She interviews her clients, retells parts of their stories, and invites her other customers to respond to the postings with their own stories and insights. This is empathy in action. This type of brand action says loud and clear to your audience, "She's interested in me, not just selling me something." Empathy, as I said before, highlights one's humility. *Victoria is not in it to win; she's in it for me.*

There are many ways to talk about who we are and highlight what we do, our accomplishments and our impact. The world we live in needs us to communicate, in words, what they can expect so they can quickly decide if they want to pay attention and invest their time and their followership in sharing your message and you. Identity, by definition, is the fact of being who or what a person or thing is. What are the facts surrounding who you are being and who you are? In personal branding, keep in mind that the goal of communicating your identity to your audience is for them to understand enough to join. But don't restrict yourself during this ongoing process. Over time, you will change, and so will your followers. Give yourself room to expand and morph; this is good for both you and for them.

Accessibility

"A brand is the set of expectations, memories, stories, and relationships that, taken together, account for a consumer's decision to choose one product or service over another."
—Seth Godin

Accessibility works in tandem with humility to control how you display your personal brand in the arena. You are the one orchestrating everything, showing up as a regular presence, interacting with people, and connecting with the wider world on your followers' behalf. You are accessible to the crowd in the nosebleed section as well as to those in the front row. Those audiences have different financial capabilities, yet they are all equals when it comes to experiencing you in the arena, and both are crucial to your brand's success. But nothing will happen unless you make yourself accessible.

Have you been hired as a private consultant to meet with a client who's highly revered in their industry? Why not ask if it's okay to press the record button during the meeting and share the video on your social platform. Imagine the vast audience this could bring in. And it's so easily done! Efforts like this give the audience access to you and to things that are normally invisible to them.

Accessible brands effectively demonstrate responsiveness to customers and consistency in messaging. They display the same characteristics to customers whenever and wherever the brand is presented, doing so through elegant marketing, audience research, and nimble adjustments to the brand when consumer preferences, resources, macroeconomics, or contexts change.

The pandemic brought to the fore the importance of using technology for access. When the lights are out in the arena, how can you maintain the spotlight on your personal brand and continue to make your content accessible?

Consider what takeaways you will leave your audience with at every connection point, whether virtual or in-person: a book you wrote, an online worksheet, a thank you email, the last newsletter you sent. Accessibility is the gift you give that makes it easy for people to act on behalf of your brand *Why*.

To be accessible, you must be technically, emotionally, and professionally available. Creating intimacy with your audience builds rapport. Think of yourself as having an ongoing conversation with your followership and network. Seeking feedback is a great way to engage and improve. Show them you are listening. Return your audience's feedback and most any kind of customer interaction with a return phone call, an email, or, better yet, a handwritten note. The more personal, the better. Quality in outreach is much more effective than quantity.

But don't wear out your followers' inboxes. Accessibility is not synonymous with copious. When you connect, come from a place of brand *Why*, tell them a bit more of your story, and inspire them. But do so in a strategic, measured way.

Introverted and Extroverted Personal Brand Building

There's a final set of characteristics to consider when it comes to defining your identity: the level of overt energy and openness you display (and receive) when you're interacting with other people. In other words, playing to whether you perceive yourself as introverted or extroverted.

I am an extrovert. Taking to the stage has been a love of mine since I was a teenager. If you are an introvert, you likely possess the superpower of being highly aware of yourself and others. Or perhaps you're an ambivert. If you're not familiar with the term, it references people with equally introverted and extroverted characteristics. The way I see it, we are actually all ambiverts, operating through varying degrees of introversion and extroversion.

You don't have to perform on stage to build your personal brand. For example, Andrew Huberman, the Stanford University scientist whom I referred to earlier in the book, was seemingly introverted. When he first came onto the scene, his humble way of presenting scientific complexities generated a mass consumer audience for his material. In his introversion, he struck people as a brilliant guy who considered his audience knowledgeable. He did not stride into the arena sporting a bold, outward personality. He did not make jokes or spin content through heavy marketing. Nor did he brag. Instead, he presented the facts surrounding his credentials—introverts are equally as inclined to personal brand building as extroverts—and this won him his now huge audience.

Every human has introverted and extroverted energy. Your best bet is to pay attention to where you are on a scale of 1–10 (1 being very introverted and 10 being highly extroverted). Are you feeling like a 10 today? Then use that extroverted energy to do something bolder than usual. Are you a 1 today? Spend time researching or recording a video of yourself in an introverted state. Use courage to help you post from a place of quiet, calm introversion and examine how powerful this is for your audience.

There is no reason not to build your personal brand on a variety of points on the introversion or extroversion spectrum. Why not explore and share your different states with your followers? And just to be clear, you certainly do not have to define yourself or your personal brand through these terms. Consider them helpful tools that can help you take effective action to show your authenticity to your audience.

There are no hard-and-fast "rules" for introverts and extroverts. Introverts can and do get on stage all the time, and they do a great job, although their presence is different than an extrovert's. They may prefer smaller arenas, or a stage consisting of a table of great thinkers they enjoy interacting with more privately. Conversely, extroverts can't be "on stage" all the time; they, too, need time in solitude. Putting yourself out there more vocally on a regular basis can become overwhelming, and insecurities may arise even in extroverts—when they do, it means they need to pause and care for their well-being.

It's up to you to activate your introverted and extroverted energy to your benefit to be consistent and honest with yourself and your audience. This is about longevity. Even the master showperson spends time in her trailer before the show.

In the context of *Influence Unleashed*, consider your arena of identity as the persona you're recognized for. By engaging in the Three Acts of Engagements, you can embody qualities like humility and accessibility, as well as shape the way you express yourself. This approach makes it simpler and more intuitive to develop a personal brand that endures over time.

PART III:

A FOUNDATION OF DISTINCTION

CHAPTER 5:

WHAT YOU "DO"—SUBJECT MATTER EXPERTISE AND THOUGHT LEADERSHIP

Now's the moment we've been building up to—exploring that unique point of distinction I've been hinting at throughout the book. In this section of the book, I invite you to join me in a deep dive, where we'll explore your expertise and relish the journey of uncovering what makes you stand out. Let's enjoy the adventure of distinguishing your personal brand together!

With the growth of my personal brand and my stature as a thought leader, I've seen a surge in invitations to speak in the media, particularly on topics like diversity, equity and inclusion, as well as on leadership and culture in the workplace. The roots of my thought leadership platform are embedded in the careful development of my personal brand, which involves identifying my core values, sharing a bold vision, and accumulating extensive expertise in the above-mentioned fields.

With a massive surge of racial and sexual discrimination events from 2020 to the current day, and their resultant social and political movements, there was a significant increase in requests for my expertise. I felt privileged to offer insightful, well-founded facts and knowledge that individuals can leverage to their and their workplace's benefit. My commitment to being strategically intentional and delivering effective communication remains steadfast because this is how I remain true to my core value of aiding people in comprehending ongoing issues and, ideally, inspiring positive change within their communities and workplaces.

There has been a proliferation of thought leadership over the last ten years. Still, upon closer examination, only a handful of thought leaders with exceptionally impactful presences have garnered the attention of millions of followers, often by focusing on a single noteworthy subject or theme. Most of them came forth as specialists in their fields.

Brené Brown, with her focused research on vulnerability, is one such example. Simon Sinek is known for helping the masses find their *Why*, Gary Vaynerchuk for revolutionizing online business marketing, and Adam Grant for his powerful insights into workplace motivation and organizational culture. Each of them burst onto the scene over the last ten years. Their messaging has inspired people to take action to such a notable extent that one could argue that they each initiated a movement.

Simon Sinek made a big splash with his viral TED Talk and his book *Start With Why*. He did an impeccable job of taking the simple concept of repeatedly asking "Why?"—originated by Sakichi Toyoda, the founder of Toyota Industries—and evolving it into an engaging conversation and tool that people could use in all facets of their lives. The Golden Circle exercise that Sinek developed begs the audience to "start with Why," showcasing that "people don't buy *what* you, they buy *why* you do it." His simple, bulls-eye drawing with Why in the centre permanently shifted how people understand and employ purpose.

There are many ways to merit the labels of "subject matter expert" and "thought leader." There's no board or agency overseeing this. If you know your field, then you can legitimately say you are a SME or thought leader—and you *should*. These labels are valuable because they serve as signposts identifying for others your area of expertise. However, the most potent strategy is to take things one step further: you must identify and curate what sets you apart and openly showcase that to the world. That can only be done through effective personal branding.

Subject Matter Expertise Defined

Subject matter expertise refers to the deep and comprehensive knowledge and understanding that an individual possesses in a particular field or domain. SMEs are recognized as authorities in their respective areas and are sought after for their insights, guidance, and problem-solving abilities.

The concept of SME has been around for centuries, as individuals have always sought out experts for advice and guidance in specialized areas. However, the formal recognition of SME emerged in the mid-20th century as organizations began to recognize the value of having in-house experts to support their decision-making processes and operational activities.

With the increasing complexity of modern industries and the rapid pace of technological change, the demand for SMEs has grown exponentially. Organizations across various sectors rely on SMEs to provide critical insights, troubleshoot complex problems, and guide innovation efforts. SMEs play a critical role in ensuring that organizations remain informed, adaptable, and responsive to the changing demands of their respective fields.

Thought Leadership Defined

Thought leadership is centred around guiding those seeking advice and direction to navigate and conquer their challenges. The difference between the two is that subject matter expertise refers to deep knowledge in a specific field, while thought leadership combines this expertise with innovative ideas and the ability to influence and inspire others in that field. Thought leaders are sometimes able to influence the direction of an entire industry.

The history of thought leadership dates back to 1994, when the term was coined by Joel Kurtzman, editor-in-chief for the magazine *Strategy and Business*. Kurtzman then wrote a book conveniently titled *Thought Leadership*, published in 1997. In it, he states, "A Thought Leader is recognized by peers, customers. and industry experts as someone who deeply understands the business they are in, the needs of their customers, and the broader marketplace in which they operate. They have distinctively original ideas, unique points of view, and new insights."

Questioning and inquiry are the engines of growth and learning. Thought leaders, like scientists, thrive on asking meaningful questions that expand their research and knowledge. One vital hallmark of expertise is the unwavering commitment to credibility in the information we disseminate.

In essence, a subject matter expert excels in a particular domain, offering depth in a specific area, whereas a thought leader offers breadth, inspiring change and new thinking in a broader context. Both roles are valuable, but they serve different purposes and have distinct impacts on their respective audiences and industries.

Establishing Credibility and Trust

"People do business with people they like and trust and, therefore, *want* to do business with." These are words that I say out loud and abide by in every moment of my professional life. When I moved into the B2B corporate world, I quickly realized that I had to learn how to make my business, team, and myself stand out in a crowded, often cut-throat industry.

If you are considered an established SME or thought leader, you likely have earned *credibility*. This is analogous to how personal branding creates *trust*. Credibility is the quality of being believable or trustworthy. It is based on evidence and facts, such as someone's expertise, experience, or track record. For example, a doctor's credibility is based on their medical training, experience, and success rates, while a scientist's credibility is based on their published research and peer review.

Trust is the belief that someone or something is reliable, honest, and well-intentioned. It is based on an emotional connection and a willingness to be vulnerable. For example, you might trust your friends to keep your secrets, even if you don't have concrete evidence of their trustworthiness.

Generally speaking, credibility is a fundamental requirement for trust. It's rare for someone perceived as lacking credibility to be trusted. Yet, it's entirely possible to be seen as credible but not trustworthy. For instance, an individual may demonstrate considerable expertise but still not earn trust if they come across as arrogant or dishonest.

Ultimately, both credibility and trust are important for building strong relationships. Credibility establishes a foundation of belief, while trust allows for deeper connection through vulnerability.

The "Easiest" Part of Building Your Personal Brand: Defining Your Expertise

The average person conducts between three and four Google searches per day. Considering this, you have a massive opportunity to be discovered by way of your subject matter expertise alone. Considering your current education, experience, and accomplishments, what keywords would you expect people to use to find you in a search engine? Think about what they need and why they are doing this search. Incorporate your findings into your brand development strategy.

In the section title above, I state that defining your area of expertise is the "easiest" part of building your personal brand. I say this because your area of expertise is largely fact and experience based; it's objectively true that you know a lot about your field and are comfortable discussing it. This baseline of competency and familiarity serves as an integral way to help you become both noticed and sought out. It increases your stature and establishes your credibility.

What is the main reason why people would seek you out? People will find you because they are looking for guidance, answers to their questions, solutions to their problems, or a trusted expert to "latch onto" in order to receive ongoing wisdom. You don't necessarily need to be a top expert in your job function or industry, but you need to be able to express with clarity what you do, why you do it, and what education and experience you bring. All of this helps to clearly define your brand and aids in your being discovered. Using your accomplishments, skills, educational experiences, and knowledge to express your thoughts and ideas with clear, relentless focus will attract your niche audience.

Developing a niche audience is an important way to begin your brand journey, which is why you want to start with leveraging your existing expertise. This expertise serves as a gateway to becoming well-known in your industry or area. I began my brand by leveraging my subject matter expertise. This foundation proved very helpful for me as I went through various industry transitions: I moved from banking operations and contact centre leadership to the outsourced contact centre industry; then I pivoted to corporate travel and from there into human capital businesses. My consistent focus throughout these transitions was on technology enablement. This became an area of subject matter expertise, and in time I evolved further from that niche into now being known for business-to-business professional services leadership and as a transformational change leader.

All of this of course wasn't exactly "easy." But my point is that by relentlessly working to build from a niche starting point, you gain traction with a highly engaged audience.

Remember that your audience will expand with you, but you have to be strategically intentional about your movements.

Start with the positive outcomes, successes, and learning that you have experienced. Identify what you want to be known for and remain committed to focusing on that in your messaging. Use the words and language that your audience would use to help them discover you—and to rank higher—in their online searches. Remember, this is a process that takes time. Any seasoned marketing professional will tell you that raising your search results ranking takes consistency, focus, and time.

Becoming a SME served as an invaluable gateway to personal branding for me. As previously defined, the journey of a SME typically commences within the confines of a specific job, industry, or organization, where they accrue in-depth knowledge and skills. Unleashing my influence was predicated on focused personal brand building. In my transition to becoming a thought leader, I likened my role to that of a scientist infused with public charisma. In my case, SME work was the springboard for my personal brand, the launchpad for me being seen and known as a thought leader. Yet, the true differentiation between being a SME and a thought leader, as opposed to mere personal branding, is found in the breadth of one's influence.

Remember that as a SME, you impact the organization or industry you are representing and working for, while thought leadership appeals to a broader audience and allows you to infuse vision into your field and inspire meaningful change.

Think of the scale of impact in terms of concentric circles: SME represents a small circle of influence, thought leadership a medium one, and personal branding the largest. It's crucial to understand that you have the choice to either operate within one of these circles or expand to encompass all three. In this book, my aim is to connect these dots for you, explaining why I am so intensely focused and passionate about the significant difference personal branding can make in terms of impact and legacy.

The Lasting Essence of You: Breaking Through Your Expertise

Think of all of the people you admire most throughout history, the people who are, in your opinion, both trustworthy and credible. In all cases, their reach would be smaller and their legacy nonexistent if they hadn't shared their lived experiences. Albert Einstein shared his spiritual views and lived experiences, including that he was late in developing his speech, made no attempt to talk until he was over the age of three, and that his parents feared he was mentally disabled. In an article in *The Washington Post* titled "Einstein, A Life," author Denis Brian relates Einstein's response to his parents' concerns: "My parents were worried because I started to talk comparatively late, and they consulted a doctor because of it. I cannot tell you how old I was at the time, but certainly not younger than three."

Had Einstein turned down the invitation to write his autobiography in 1949, he would have left the world with E=mc2 and his Nobel Prize, but much else about the man behind the crazy, grey lightning-struck hairdo would have remained a mystery. Doesn't it make Einstein's life so much more interesting and relatable to your own experience knowing that he didn't pass his college entrance exam, that he was born with a misshapen head, and that a compass his father gave him at the age of 5 may be the foundation on which he discovered the Theory of Relativity? Would the masses be interested in him enough to buy T-shirts with his face on them that feature famous quotes of his like "Imagination is more important than knowledge" and "I want to know God's thoughts . . . the rest are details"? I think not. If Einstein had remained known to us only through his scientific discoveries, he would not have engaged our common humanity in the way he did. He would have seemed one dimensional.

An accomplished genius with life stories that mirror ours makes it seem like maybe we can discover something unique too, that maybe whatever we want to accomplish *is* possible and that no matter the shape of our head, we can think big and leave our own legacy of accomplishments and life stories behind.

CHAPTER 6:

WHAT MAKES YOU, YOU?

In May of 2023, I travelled to Italy and fell in love with the country. In many of my interviews, I exclaim that I am particularly passionate about wine, of which Italy has a wonderful abundance. While I could tell you all about my love of wine, I would instead like to acknowledge someone who translated his very same passion into a powerful personal brand.

Gary Vaynerchuk has been all over social media for years. He is widely recognized for his thought leadership in the world of digital marketing and social media as the chairman of New York–based communications company VaynerX, and as CEO of VaynerX subsidiary VaynerMedia. But long before any of these entrepreneurial pursuits existed, he was a wine critic who built a steadfast following on his YouTube channel, "Wine Library TV," which he started when YouTube was less than a year old. This early, innovative channel helped his family's wine business, Wine Library, explode.

In today's hyperconnected world, storytelling is pivotal in shaping and connecting our perceptions. The digital age has provided unprecedented platforms for sharing stories, enabling us to reach audiences far beyond geographical boundaries. Vaynerchuk strategically used digital media and the advent of YouTube to grow his family's business, but the key to his success was his terrific ability to relate stories to his audience.

"Hello, everybody and welcome to Wine Library TV. I am your host, Gary Vaynerchuk. This, my friends, is the thunder show, aka the internet's most passionate wine program." On the ten-year anniversary of Wine Library TV, Vaynerchuk filmed episode 1001 to commemorate the occasion. This particular episode came after episode 1000, which had been filmed five years prior.

The dazzling thing about watching Vaynerchuk taste premium wines is that he is so obviously in his seat of passion. His voice and his mannerisms position the fine wines he tastes as being accessible to everyone, despite their high quality. He tastes them in the midst of conversations he has with his audience about mundane things such as his love of the New York Jets, or during discussions where he shares his various rather unique ideas about what to do with wine, such as pairing it with cereal. No wonder Wine Library has been so incredibly successful. Driven with passion that screams authenticity, Vaynerchuk has offered his expertise and his personality to the world. And the world has most heartily accepted him.

Crafting a great story requires meshing very personal ingredients, such as your passions, interests, and lived experiences. Vaynerchuk talks to his audience about being a child buying and selling sports cards, about his love of football and desire to buy the New York Jets. He doesn't tell us these stories about himself because he's selfish or self-absorbed. It's a gift he gives to others, a gift that creates a powerful and lasting connection.

When you consider your own "hook," think about it as your connection point. I am a wife, mother, and fitness fanatic who has played ice hockey for 20 years. When I tell people about my interests, almost always they connect to at least one of them. We break the ice, engage, and come to know one another on some level. When I share what I'm extremely committed to being—the things that are driven by my core values—others share theirs with me and there's a sense that we are both operating with integrity. Trust is formed.

In this age of information overload and constant distractions, crafting meaningful and engaging personal brand narratives has become more crucial than ever. The attention economy, where companies and individuals vie for people's attention, demands a strategic approach to storytelling that resonates with audiences and leaves a lasting impression. Vaynerchuk is the perfect example of showing who you are by, over time, offering to your audience small helpings of the thousands of details that make up who you are. Watching him, you get an idea of the kind of person he is, and I would venture to say that he did a damn good job of getting people to feel like he's the sort of guy they would love to hang out with, watch football with, and maybe even trade in that tall mug of beer for a glass of premium wine. He uses humour and candor (and a whole lot of swear words!) to display who he is to his audience and engage people in tasting wine in a totally fresh and distinctive way.

Vaynerchuk's so honest in his assessment of the wines as he examines them, so clearly confident and well-trained as a wine expert, so unapologetic about giving his opinion. Watching an episode is a truly unique experience that includes learning, some laughing, and coming away with the pleasant feeling that you are with someone who you would want to have over to your home. He makes you want to taste wine.

Every element of Wine Library TV screams passion—even the New York Jets-branded wine spit bucket stands out, magnifying his personality by expressing his devotion to his favourite sports team.

Obviously Gary's strategy has paid off, and not just in terms of his huge social influence. According to an article on business2community.com, "Gary Vaynerchuk, better known as Gary Vee, is a multimillionaire, a successful entrepreneur, a highly paid consultant, and the founder and CEO of several companies. As of 2023, Gary Vaynerchuk's net worth is estimated at $300 million."

In what ways might you be similar to Gary? Can you emulate what he did? Can you discover that sweet spot of expertise where your skills and fervour intersect, enriched by your unique interests, passions, and personal experiences—that spot where you can craft a brand that resonates deeply with your audience? This alignment paves the way for a multitude of opportunities to broaden and enhance your personal brand.

Remember that those who embrace your personal brand should reap its rewards. Like Vaynerchuk, you're already a one-of-a-kind value proposition in action, but truly understanding the value of *you* will require effort, patience, experimentation, and consistency. It's like building muscle at the gym—you can't skip the critical elements for growth. To continue building muscle, you need to continually challenge your muscles with more weight or resistance. That's what we are doing here together, strengthening the power of your personal brand over time so it stands the test of time.

PART IV:

LONGEVITY AND LEGACY OF YOUR BRAND

CHAPTER 7:

BUILDING A BRAND OF DISTINCTION: YOUR UNIQUE VALUE PROPOSITION

Years ago, I was preparing to compete in a bodybuilding competition. Spending significant time at the gym every day, I noticed a woman who was there even longer than I was to work out. Her muscular physique and bulging veins made it clear that she was more than a fitness fanatic; she was a bodybuilder. Curious to know more about her experience, I asked her if she was, in fact, training for a competition. She confirmed that she was and a conversation ensued.

After a post-workout meeting, we connected on social media. Within a year, as I embarked on a new role, I discovered she was one of my clients. Our professional relationship quickly blossomed into a friendship, and she became an invaluable guide for me to learn about and get connected to people within her company. Her introducing me to a publisher led to my first coauthorship opportunity. Now, our roles have reversed and she's my client, seeking my expertise in executive and public speaking coaching. Our mutual interest in fitness was the catalyst for this effortless connection. This experience underscores how shared passions can foster unexpected and fruitful connections. Often, the most meaningful relationships emerge organically when you engage with others who share your interests.

It had never occurred to me that exercise and fitness—such an important but routine part of my life—might provide the basis for a meaningful connection. When it comes to personal branding, sometimes our biggest points of distinction are overlooked by us because they are so close to us. You may be immersed so deeply in something you are passionate about or interested in that you miss the part where you connect the dots that ultimately lead to you standing out from others. Sure, there are plenty of other fitness enthusiasts out there, but my fitness background plays into the way I stand on stage, the strength I have in enduring and overcoming challenges, and the heavy lifts I have taken on in transforming businesses.

Points of Distinction

When it comes to branding, your distinctiveness must be forward-facing. It must be a repeating theme in your story and present in all contexts of your life. While there may be new and different versions of the words or phrases that you choose, and while your brand's stories may evolve, they should never lose the authenticity which is so crucial to the ongoing development of your personal brand-building efforts. If you are serious about the business of your personal brand, then you have come to realize that you must offer something distinctive to consumers.

Why should anyone choose you over one of your competitors? What makes your brand more appealing to them than the other candidates, consultants, or experts? What facet of your character and unique story helps you boldly stand out? Your answers to these questions begin to shape your distinctiveness in brand development.

Distinctiveness, also called uniqueness, is never about arrogance; it's always about authenticity. Distinctiveness is not the story you wish you had or the false narrative you'd prefer to convey to the world instead of the real deal. Distinctiveness is your story and your story alone. As I've mentioned before, each of us is a distinct blend of life experiences, personality traits, viewpoints, and personal history. If you doubt that there's anything distinct about you, rest assured, every person on this planet has many points of distinction. The challenge in developing your brand is allowing that uniqueness to shine through by putting it out there.

In the competitive marketplace, where brands vie for attention and loyalty, a unique value proposition (UVP) stands as a beacon of differentiation, clearly articulating what sets you apart from the crowd. It's the essence of your brand, the promise of value that resonates with your target audience and compels them to choose you over your competitors.

It takes courage to stand out in this way. We all feel some level of discomfort when we don't "fit in." I remember how in my early 20s, when my colleagues gave me the moniker of The Iron Maiden at work, I had been doing what I thought I needed to do to fit in. Fitting in reminds me of squeezing into a pair of too-tight jeans. In terms of leadership, that can look like a muffin top of valuable parts of our core, keeping us uncomfortable as we try to hide it rather than just wear a pair of jeans that fit. The thinking that our stories are too little or too much may hold us back from finding a connection with our audience. But to truly belong means there's room for all of us, including the qualities that make us all unique. The audience sees and feels the comfort in that, and they will ask you for more once your point of distinction is clear. If you can't breathe, you are fitting in. Take notice of the fit.

Navigating the Essence of a Unique Value Proposition

A UVP is not merely a marketing tagline or a clever catchphrase; it's a deep understanding of your brand's core strengths and the unique benefits you offer that address specific customer needs and pain points, all while simultaneously making progress on your goals. It answers the fundamental question: "Why should someone invest their attention and engage with your content over another?"

To uncover your brand's UVP, let's embark on a journey of introspection, delving into the heart of your brand's identity, its values, and the problems you solve for your customers. You are well on your way already.

Step 1: Unveil Your UVP: A Journey of Discovery

Part of my UVP is telling clients and others what they need to hear, not what they want to hear. I also say no to things that aren't aligned with my core values. I say no to clients if matters aren't aligned, or in the name of doing the right thing. I say no to opportunities that I believe would negatively impact the longevity of my brand. A company who had suffered PR nightmares because of their discriminatory practices to both employees and customers hired my company to develop a DEI strategy and communication plan. I was asked to lead the engagement, given my DEI expertise and strength communicating to C-suite executives. After multiple conversations, I felt they wanted a performative act, pretending to fix the problem by slapping a mask over their policies, leadership actions, language, and behaviour. They weren't really committed to changing. This was not for me. That is not the work I do, and no amount of money will compromise my integrity. This forms a substantial component of what makes me different. So I politely told these executives I could no longer help them and moved on.

I stand my ground in a world of compromised morals, values, and beliefs. My audience is moved to stand theirs. That is the movement I want for you and your brand, too. No amount of money will make you as satisfied as you are when you stand tall for who you are and what makes you different. And maintaining your integrity is about more than your being able to live with yourself: it's strategically crucial for the health of your brand. A brand without integrity is a brand that will inevitably alienate its followers and fail to stand the test of time.

Identifying your UVP requires deep understanding and confidence in yourself, your followership, and your knowledge of the competitive landscape. Here's a road map to guide your UVP discovery process:

1. **Reflect on Your Unique Experiences and Skills:** Think about your background, experiences, and skills that are distinct to you. What have you done that most others haven't? This could include unique career

paths, life experiences, skills acquired, or even your approach to problem-solving.

2. **Identify Your Personal Brand's Core Values:** What values drive you? Often, your differentiation lies in the values that you stand for. This could be a commitment to innovation, a passion for social change, or a dedication to excellence in your field.

3. **Understand Your Audience's Needs and Preferences:** Knowing what your audience values, struggles with, and aspires to can help you tailor your differentiation. How can your unique attributes meet these needs or address these pain points?

4. **Analyze Your Competition:** Look at others in your space. What are they known for? Identifying gaps in what they offer compared to your unique skills and experiences can help you find your niche.

5. **Articulate Your Unique Offer:** Combine your unique skills, experiences, and values with your audience's needs to formulate a clear statement that captures what sets you apart. This statement should be concise and easy to communicate (see step 2, below).

6. **Showcase Real-Life Examples:** Use stories and examples from your life or career that illustrate your unique qualities. This not only makes your differentiation more tangible, but also more relatable and memorable.

Step 2: Create Your UVP Statement

Now that you've gone through step 1 and gathered the various raw elements that make up your brand identity, it's time to formalize them. Your unique value proposition is a concise statement articulating your distinctive value to your audience. It should clearly explain how you can help them solve their problems and achieve their goals.

Fill in the blanks in the form below with words that describe your UVP. Use decisive- and action-oriented language to make your statement compelling. Please consider this form to be nothing more than a guidance-offering template; feel free to change it up and make it your own. Go ahead and insert different describing words. Figure out what works for you so that the process will yield a true expression of your UVP. I think you will find this to be a useful exercise for helping you communicate the concepts we've so far covered in this book: what you do (expertise), who you are (lived experiences), your passion, interests, values, and the value you create for others:

As a [your profession or title], I help [your target audience] achieve [their desired outcome] by [your unique method or approach] that [the results you generate] through [how you do it]. I am [your strongest skill or attribute] and [your second-strongest skill or trait]. I am committed to [what you value]. I am passionate about [your area of expertise] and committed to helping my clients [achieve their goals].

83

Example:

As a seasoned executive, board director, and keynote speaker, I specialize in transforming large businesses through the cultivation of high-performing teams and fostering positive organizational cultures. I am relentlessly committed to my core values: integrity, radical candor, and Whole Human Leadership, emphasizing authenticity and empathy. I'm deeply passionate about advancing Diversity, Equity, and Inclusion, and committed to helping my clients understand the moral implications and positive business results, not just within the workplace but in broader societal contexts as well.

Once you've developed the first draft of your UVP, I recommend that you don't immediately broadcast it to the world. Take some time refining it. Think about it. Share it with friends or trusted colleagues to get their feedback. Practice saying your UVP out loud. Does it feel different when you verbalize it? Like your personal brand, expect to refine your UVP over time as you test it and gain feedback.

Step 3: Test Your UVP: The Proof Is in the Traction

"You are an iconic hire, Victoria." The senior executive for one of the global corporations I worked for said this to me the moment after I accepted the position. What a difference between this and that long-ago interview I shared earlier with you when I fumbled for the words to define what was unique about me (and failed to get the position). By now, my UVP has been known to the public for a number of years—and at some point, you'll be ready to come forward with yours. When you do, be sure to do what I did: test your UVP, analyze the results, and keep going until you have evidence of its traction and success.

Traction is the point of investment. This can mean something impactful, like being hired for a position or asked to speak at a conference, or something as simple as being approached by people asking permission to share your content. The investment has to match up with your goals to matter; once it does, the flywheel releases.

Validating your UVP—otherwise known as making sure your audience is experiencing what you think they are experiencing—can be a very rewarding part of building and finessing your personal brand. The most exciting thing in personal branding is when it comes alive. Gathering feedback from people who are reading, watching, and engaging with your personal brand takes another bout of courage. But it's well worth it. This is where you get to be the scientist of your brand. What's working? What's not resonating? What do your followers want to see more of? This also gives you even more credibility and trust between you and your audience because it proves to them that you are *interested in them*—and that breeds engagement.

The Consistency of Your Brand of Distinction

There isn't a different version of me in business versus my personal life. I share slightly different pictures of elements based on the platform and audience, but it is always all me. Your uniqueness shines through in your capacity to acknowledge and set aside what you're not, enabling you to concentrate on what truly brings you purpose. By sharing your authentic story with strategic intent, you distinguish yourself in a meaningful way.

Uncovering your unique value proposition is a journey of self-discovery, mining your lived experiences for the gems of wisdom and expertise that set you apart. By delving into your personal narrative, identifying pain points, crafting a compelling UVP, and sharing your story with impact, you can transform your personal branding efforts into a powerful force for positive impact. As you embark on this journey, remember that your UVP is not static; it will evolve as you grow and learn, and as your goals and objectives change, it will reflect your ever-expanding horizons and deepening impact.

CHAPTER 8:

LEGACY AND IMPACT

"It's not sacrifice, it's family." These five words are embroidered on the inside of one of Ruth Bader Ginsburg's (RBG) famous collars given to her by her late husband, Marty Ginsburg. Every layer of material making up this particular collar represents a different family member of RBG.

The collection of distinctive collars, or jabots, that RGB has left behind are material representations of the impact she made during her life and the rich legacy she left behind. Surprisingly, Supreme Court Justices do not have to adhere to a dress code. The plain black robes they wear today are simply an honoured tradition. Maintaining the tradition, RBG wore her black robe on August 10th, 1993, the first time she took to the bench, but you might say she added a bit more flare to the monotone ensemble. Adding dissent on top of history, RBG and Justice Sandra Day O'Connor wore white lace jabots to set themselves apart from their male colleagues. It was a quietly bold move, typical of RBG, that would be a significant symbol of the legacy she would leave behind. As the second woman to sit on the Supreme Court, her collection grew as her personal brand grew, representing her lived experiences, expertise, passion, interests, and values. Every one of her jabots carries significant meaning and her collars were a hallmark of her presence through time.

Defining Legacy and Impact

Impact is the effect or influence that someone or something has on someone or something. It can be positive, negative, or neutral. I would add to this that it happens while you are living, can officially begin at any moment you so choose, and expands over time with a well-followed personal brand.

Ruth Bader Ginsburg was an American lawyer and jurist who served as an associate justice of the Supreme Court of the United States from 1993 to 2020, known for her strong support of gender equality. Holding an extremely authoritative position like Ginsberg is not a requirement to create impact. Every human can have influence, if they so choose, and every one of us can impact the world around us. I always say that if I can make a positive impact in one person's life, it is worth the effort.

Ginsburg had a significant impact on American law and society. Earlier in her career, she had argued six cases before the Supreme Court that all resulted in victories for women's rights. In addition to her work on gender equality, Ginsburg was also a strong advocate for civil rights and liberties.

Making an impact is about leaving a positive mark on the world and making a difference in the lives of others. It can be done through big or small acts, and it doesn't require any special skills or talents. What it does require is action.

Legacy is the enduring influence of someone or something. Positive, negative, or neutral, legacy can be the result of a single event or a lifetime of actions both large or small. Individuals, organizations, or even entire societies create legacies that can be tangible or intangible, physical or abstract. A source of inspiration and pride, a legacy can be a reminder of the importance of making a positive impact on the world.

After Ginsburg's death, *TIME Magazine* published an article on her collection of collars. The remarkable pieces she left behind, an anthology of tangible objects that represented her expression of individuality and courage, remind us of the work she did that challenged the traditional norms of society. From her rainbow-beaded "Pride Collar," representing her work as a champion for the LGBTQ+ community, to the "Majority Collar" she wore when announcing a majority opinion from the bench, to the collar she wore representing her love of the opera, her legacy is a marriage of who she was and what she did, and even includes her interests. RBG has now left the Earth . . . but has she? She is on coffee mugs and T-shirts, still makes the news, and her documentary is available to stream. Two years ago, I dressed up as RBG for Halloween. While this might not seem relevant to legacy, it absolutely is. RBG's personal brand is standing the test of time because she was able to transcend generational gaps, and part of that was the adoration of her work through pop culture making her an icon.

The work you have done so far in reading this book has been designed to serve as the base for you to step in to take action to create your legacy. Everyone can leave a legacy. Think about the elders in your family. Perhaps your grandmother left behind her journals, recipes that are beloved by your family, and photos of life during World War II. Maybe she was known for volunteering at the local shelter, a picture of her doing so forever posted to the wall.

A legacy forms from acting on behalf of our expertise, lived experiences, passions, interests, and core values, and, no matter how small or large your reach, it is going to be impactful on someone. I was adopted and have limited information about my biological family and was never close with my adoptive parents' extended family, so my own family legacy is relatively unknown. In my experience, that is all the more reason to create one and or to break the cycle of history and circumstance.

Asking yourself great questions, regularly, can help you define your legacy:

- What do you want to be remembered for?

- What do you want people to say about you after you are gone?

- If you died tomorrow, how would you have left the world a better place?

- What values have you championed throughout your life?

- What do you advocate for?

- Who have you mentored?

Your impact and legacy include your achievements, but are so much more than them. Do you remember many other Supreme Court Justices as fondly as RBG? There's a reason for that. She was courageous enough to be herself and use her voice to promote the impact she wanted to make while she was alive, and to form the expansive legacy that would inspire generations to come to stand up to inequality.

Communicating Your Legacy

In his book *The 8th Habit: From Effectiveness to Greatness*, Stephen Covey introduces the concept of "Find your voice and inspire others to find theirs" as the eighth habit, building upon the foundation of the previous seven habits he articulated in *The 7 Habits of Highly Effective People*. Covey emphasizes that effectiveness, while crucial, is not sufficient to achieve greatness. Greatness, he argues, stems from finding one's unique voice and using it to inspire others to discover their own voices.

If there's one thing that Andrew Huberman, Gary Vaynerchuk, Simon Sinek, and others with leading personal brands have in common, it is that they have found their voice and, more importantly, they are courageous in using it. Without this courage, there would be no coffee mug quotes or social media presence. But on top of that, their voices and their courage have the effect Covey describes: they inspire others to find their own voices.

At the heart of the 8th Habit lies the concept of "voice," which Covey defines as the "unique personal significance" that each individual possesses. This voice is not simply about being heard or expressing oneself; it's about understanding one's deep-seated values, passions, and purpose. By discovering their voice, individuals can live with greater authenticity, conviction, and impact. I would argue that your voice is synonymous with the impact you want to make through the *Why* of your brand and the legacy you want to leave behind.

My hope is that you understand how using your voice provokes the change you want to see in the world, albeit with the knowledge that the impact you make may not come to full fruition while you are alive.

Currently, my oldest child is almost 24 years old, and I espouse to him often what I do so vocally with others, instilling the importance of why every college graduate should launch out of school with a personal brand strategy based on the use of their voice. While it's highly unlikely they will take the reins at that young of an age, it's important to acknowledge that when you find your voice you help others find theirs. Gaining clarity on what you define or consider the impact you want to make will set you up with the foundation that supports dramatic change, potentially for generations to come.

When F. Scott Fitzgerald died in 1940, he considered himself a failure. *The Great Gatsby*, his landmark novel, was commercially unsuccessful. He died with royalties totalling just $13. In 1941, only approximately a year after his death, *The Great Gatsby* was chosen to be donated to World War II troops overseas. F. Scott Fitzgerald's voice, through Gatsby, entered the lives of millions of men returning from war. The adulation didn't stop there. As a result of the success of *Gatsby*, Fitzgerald's short stories were republished and the rest, as they say, is history.

More than likely you have in some way experienced *The Great Gatsby*, even if you didn't read the book. The novel was made into a movie starring Leonardo DiCaprio, people host Gatsby theme parties at their homes, and the book's cultural echoes continue to be heard. For those who have read the book, its themes of social commentary on the flaws of the American Dream are still brought to mind.

While it may be heartbreaking to think that F. Scott Fitzgerald did not see the apex of his success, it is admirable that he committed to using his voice and building his life's work publicly, leaving us with his legacy. You do not know what your legacy will bring, but if you stop creating it, you will have a basement (or a Google Drive) full of artefacts. Your voice gives impact and legacy legs.

Aligning Values and Action

Aligning your actions and values is an essential step toward living a meaningful and fulfilling life. When your actions are consistent with your deeply held beliefs, you experience a sense of authenticity, purpose, and inner peace. However, identifying and addressing contradictions between your actions and values can be a challenging process.

Employing the Three Acts of Engagement will help you take a good look in the mirror on the regular to continually identify where you are in terms of alignment and where you need an adjustment. In the documentary *RGB*, you will see how aligned Ruth Bader Ginsberg was in all areas of her life. She woke up at 4 am every day, a mother of two committed to her family and her work. She embraced every single role she took on until the moment she passed away. We can all aspire to be like RBG, unwavering in our value systems.

Earlier in the book, we began the process of defining your core values by understanding how they connect with passion and lived experiences. Now, it's time to dig in deeper to uncover that sense of purpose and fulfillment that living according to your core values creates. Doing so requires self-reflection. Take some time for introspection to identify the principles and beliefs that guide your life. These are your core values, which serve as the foundation for your decisions and actions. Consider what matters most to you, what qualities you admire, and what principles you want to uphold.

On a more challenging note, it's time to reflect on your current actions. Examine the way you are living your life. Your daily routine, habits, and decision-making patterns *show* whether you are aligned or not. To avoid feeling shame around your current actions, which perhaps are out of alignment with your values, I recommend that you look at yourself objectively. If you say you never bend on your healthy eating regimen, as an example, but you go through the fast-food drive-through once a week, you have a choice: you can either alter your narrative about yourself, or you can alter your behaviour. But something needs to change. It is detrimental to be out of alignment for too long. The important thing is to make it true to your way of being to avoid feeling and looking like a fraud or a walking contradiction. Acknowledge the disconnects and then identify what you need to do and say to course correct and get your backbone straight.

It often requires courage to take an honest look at yourself. But the truth will set you free, helping you make more conscious choices through clearer self-awareness. Over time, your choices will become more automatic. You will feel proud of the way you are showing up, even if it means a short-term loss. I promise, living by your core values will not disappoint you or your audience who trusts you.

There was a time when I boldly and professionally (the two can go together, you know) pulled myself out of the recruitment process for a company where the CEO clearly demonstrated that he wasn't prepared for change and transformation. Maybe he had good intentions, but his actions communicated that *his* core values were not truly in line with him saying that he wanted transformation and greater diversity in his leadership team. After he continued to hire people that looked like him and came from his former employer, it was clear to me that if I remained in the running for the position, I would likely be challenged in achieving the desired outcomes he sought and potentially pressured to compromise my core values. Sticking to your guns like this might sound scary, but it's the opposite. It's an accountability system that prevents misalignments and conflicts that will eventually steer you off course if you bend. RBG was relentless in sticking to her core values, and that's how she got things done, built bridges, and stood for something beyond her position.

You are your own executive, the CEO of your life. So like a good CEO, be strategic with how you go about expanding your impact and legacy. Set goals and establish metrics to help track your progress and make sure you stay accountable and on track. Putting in this sort of framework will provide volumes of useful data in terms of informing you if you are, in fact, walking the walk. If you miss the mark, you are likely out of alignment. Having a great foundation built on goals and clearly articulated intentions will help you direct the flight path of your impact and legacy.

Goals help create accountability, but if you don't share them with anyone, the odds of you making the impact you want to make lessens. Having support systems in place with people who share your values helps create a stronger backbone. It's usual to have moments when you need to phone a person who really understands you, who is there to help you stand in courage, vulnerability, and authenticity.

Aligning your actions and values is an ongoing process, and there are always going to be at least small imbalances. Regularly reflect on your progress and make adjustments as needed. Be patient with yourself and celebrate your achievements. Pay attention to your emotions: Notice when you feel conflicted, guilty, or regretful after making a decision or taking an action. These emotions may indicate a misalignment between your actions and values.

And *never* fail to consider the impact of your actions: Think about the consequences of your choices on yourself, others, and the world around you. Are your actions contributing to positive outcomes or causing harm?

Seek feedback from trusted friends and mentors: Ask people you respect for their honest perspectives on your actions and how well they align with your values. Reflect on your values regularly: Keep your core values at the forefront of your mind. Regularly revisit your values list to ensure your actions are consistent with your beliefs.

The Constant Unfolding of Impact and Legacy

Like the first day Ginsburg donned one of her collars, the strategic intention that you have for your personal brand is made with the first conscious action you take toward building it. And, keep in mind that your personal brand will transform over time. RGB's first collar was like a test of expression. People started to notice this signature mark and learned the meaning behind it, and they continued to follow her as her experiences unfolded, along with her collars.

Impact and legacy are interwoven with who you are, what you do, and your passions, interests, and core values—these all feed into the *Why* of your personal brand. Impact and legacy are the elements that are likely to change most often as you build your personal brand because they are dependent on your experiences and influenced by the world around you. I mentioned earlier that I had been called upon in 2020 to speak up more often in the media about DEI due to the social climate. This was a macro social calling that I did not expect but that I was prepared for, and which ultimately deepened the layer of my personal brand associated with DEI. Prepare yourself for such possibilities by diligently working through everything we have covered so far. Doing this work will help you discover how impact and legacy show up and transform over time.

When I was promoted into leadership very early in my career, I thought of success as a position, title, and compensation level. Over time my definition of success matured as I grew as a person, learning to experience more joy in my life, and feeling the pride and satisfaction of seeing the rise and success of my team. Today, my aim is to create a legacy shaped by my personal journey, turning the hurdles I've faced and the lessons I've learned into stepping stones for triumph. By demonstrating how to surmount these challenges, I aspire to inspire others to do the same. But it doesn't stop there. My quest has evolved into a commitment to enhance the workplace culture of every organization I touch, striving to leave it in a better state than I found it. This journey has sparked in me a desire to champion a new breed of leadership, one rooted in empathy and authenticity. Embracing and embodying this style of leadership, I'm passionate about promoting what I term Whole Human Leadership. Walking the walk when it came to Whole Human Leadership meant that I became a leader for social injustice, an advocate for women and the LGBTQ+ community, and a branding coach and mentor, so that I could help others make an impact too.

Your Contribution

Everyone has something distinct to contribute to the world that will fuel impact and define legacy. Too often, we miss recognizing that the small moments or private interactions we share with people are themselves contributions. We all tend to think that impact and legacy are grandiose. While they can be, it may be a relief to you to understand that impact and legacy are built by stacking behaviours over time.

Creating impact and legacy, your contributions that last, are gifts to the world and often happen when we expect nothing in return. In the book *Never Eat Alone*, Keith Ferrazzi talks about the power of building your network when you don't need anything. I always consider that to be important when it comes to impact and legacy.

"Mary, I am always happy to hear from you, but I have to be honest with you: the last three times you reached out to me was because you wanted something from me. I want to help you, but I also want you to know that it doesn't read well for our relationship." My commitment to being radically candid was a gift to Mary when I told her how I felt about the nature of her outreach. I wanted to contribute my perspective to help her realize that her communication with her network—in this case, me—read inauthentic and greedy because she seemed to reach out only when she had "an ask." Everything a truly great leader does comes from a place of generosity, and gifts aren't always wrapped up in a pretty bow. I know my "gift" to Mary wasn't; but I do believe it was necessary. Contributions can feel risky, especially when you are looking to make a difference.

When I realized the vast contradiction between The Iron Maiden moniker I was given and the resilient, heart-centred person my closest friends knew me to be, it was evident that I was not acting in alignment with the leader I wanted to become and the legacy I envisioned leaving behind.

I'm known as a connector and a person who contributes to the growth of others. That means that I commit to making sure that I unleash my influence to help others do the same. Through employing my core value of radical candor with Mary, I believe I left behind an impression with her of the importance of coming forward with generosity.

Contribution and legacy are often equated with monetary gifts. We see park benches with placards with a donor's name on them, or a philanthropic, nonprofit foundation created in someone's name supported by their trust. While financial contributions are important, when it comes to personal branding, I recommend that you come from a place of giving your expertise, lived experiences, passions, interests, and core values. If you do that, the money might well follow, but in my experience the rewards that come from leaving the world a better place are exponentially more satisfying.

The Will to Keep Going

I have focused on building my personal brand for over 20 years. Turning away from being the Iron Maiden at work was the first of many pivots I have had to make, and probably one of the easiest, if I am being honest. In so many ways, being authentic and vulnerable, and adhering to my core values, has benefited me immensely, and I would do all that I've done over and over again.

It's important to tell you that along with the success I have had, there has also been a lot of adversity in the process. That's why courage is so central to personal brand-building. Putting yourself out there because you believe in something bigger than yourself that can spring from your lived experiences, skills, and expertise is hard work. As you recognize what takes shape around you, your definition of success may grow into something much broader than its original formulation. "I see you everywhere!" a woman at a recent networking event said to me. When people recognize me and automatically know what I stand for, I realize that all of the pivoting and hurdle jumping has paid off. It's not about the woman recognizing me like some type of celeb thought leader, it's about her recognizing that she sees herself in me, even if our stories are different, because she's faced challenges and adversity too.

If I hadn't begun a focused effort around building my personal brand, I'm not sure that I would be able to so clearly articulate the values, beliefs, and purpose that make up my identity. Moreover, I would have little to no idea what type of impact I could make and what legacy I would want to leave behind. What has been reflected back to me—good, bad, and ugly—has driven me to face down any inconsistencies and contradictions in the name of unleashing my influence. You know you have something to say that is important, and the best way that you can get better at understanding how to deliver that something is through doing it out loud. Personal brand building, whether you are introverted or extroverted, is about sharing, so when I say "out loud," I don't mean standing up on stage like I do. I mean making yourself heard in whatever manner works for you. The only thing that doesn't work is holding it all in.

No matter how old you are, it's time to begin, because even though a particular Instagram post might go viral overnight, it doesn't automatically convert to sales. Nor does networking. Developing your brand takes time. No matter where you are at in your willingness to activate your qualities of courage, vulnerability, and authenticity, it will take consistent and ongoing practice to make progress. I know very courageous, vulnerable, and authentic people who reached the pinnacle of their success only after years of showing up that way. When you enter the Arena of Identity, share from a place of generosity, and meet your audience at the intersection of their story and yours. Your UVP will come alive and your audience will engage for the long haul.

I haven't previously mentioned this, but I do private coaching for executives, working with a select few clients at a time. At the start of developing their personal brand with them,

I always stress how important it is to understand that there are results below the surface of yourself and your audience that you will not see overnight. Maintaining your commitment, and continually analyzing and practicing everything we have gone over in this book, will pay off if you are willing to stay the course.

PART V:

PUTTING IT
ALL TOGETHER

CHAPTER 9:

PUTTING YOUR BRAND INTO ACTION

Are you consistently acting like the leader you aspire to be, or do you believe that you have already "arrived"? Consistently taking action and being aware of the results of your actions will protect you from becoming known as a one-hit wonder leader who is on message one minute and off the next.

The idea of a one-hit-wonder seems relevant to me when it comes to leadership. The path to becoming distinctive is not through having one song that gets a lot of plays but is then relegated to the archives. Wouldn't it be better to end up on people's mixtapes, or to have a gold album version with all your greatest hits? Looking at everything you do as a potential great hit will help you identify the unique value you create for your audience through time. One-hit wonder songs almost always play a different tone and personality than the rest of the album. According to the listener, everything is right with that song, but the rest of the album doesn't quite match up. Your personal branding tone and personality have to align in every area of your life for you to become a leader that people want to follow.

Who wants to follow inconsistency or inaction? If you show up one day as one person and the next day as another, your audience will need continual clarification and your messaging will fail to create an impact. Consistency in your delivery, beliefs, and actions compounds over time, not overnight. In your work life, where you're articulating a brand, you should see yourself as a leader. To tell a great story, you have to own it and lead.

Leadership is not in title or hierarchy alone. Everyone can be a leader. Some people are born with innate characteristics of a leader, but few achieve perfect leadership without nurturing skills over time. This requires bias to action. When all else fails, do one small thing that will move the needle.

Too often, we reduce leadership to a list of skills one must possess to manage a group of followers, or we simply define it by stereotypical hierarchies. An effective leader is a great communicator, planner, teacher, intellectual, or tactician. Sometimes, we equate leadership with that one great meeting or speech, but how quickly does your audience forget if you are not consistently showing up? Maya Angelou may stand out for her first book, *I Know Why the Caged Bird Sings,* but her words have reverberated through time as her unique style has impacted the world over and over again. She went on to become a leader of the civil rights movement, working with Dr. Martin Luther King Junior and Malcolm X, and she made approximately 80 public appearances per year. Her accomplishments could easily take up the entirety of this book. And it all began with that first, deeply personal book that moved the world to want more and more of the overwhelming value she was creating.

Leadership is the culmination of the 18-inch active journey from one's head to one's heart, travelling from what you do to who you are. This is the path where you will discover your unique value proposition, the point of audience investment and the preliminary work it takes to develop the narrative arc of your brand.

There's so much agency that comes with leadership, *and* so much responsibility. Through personal brand building, you can take your conversations forward by demonstrating with your actions that you are the change you want to see in the world.

The number of calls I received for expert media experiences in 2020 and beyond would have been much less without the social unrest. Since the beginning of my personal brand building, I have been openly queer and advocating for women, but it wasn't until issues of equality, workforce burnout, and discrimination began to rise to the surface that my personal brand was called upon more publicly.

Chances are, it's going to take a while before you start noticing the fruits of your labour, given the multitude of elements involved in bringing your personal brand to life. Dealing with inertia can be quite a test of patience, but rest assured, even the tiniest steps you're making now are building momentum, often in ways you'll only realize later on. Rosa Parks didn't start standing up for her rights that day on the bus. Dr. Martin Luther King Jr. didn't launch his legacy with his famous "I Have a Dream" speech. Both were taking actions daily before they became famous for the single act you may associate with them today.

Acting now puts your brand into action today and prepares you and your audience for the day that your messaging is needed the most. Brené Brown spent years researching vulnerability, unknowingly preparing herself to speak on the

TED stage and become a famous expert on the topic. Her years of behind-the-scenes consistent effort led her to become an enduring influencer in her field.

The Influence of the Social and Economic Climate on Action

The social and economic climate can create moments of momentum for personal branding in several ways. First, it can raise awareness of specific issues or trends, providing individuals with an opportunity to position themselves as experts in those areas. For example, the rise of environmental consciousness has created a demand for experts in sustainability and green living. Individuals who have established themselves as authorities in these areas can leverage this momentum to expand their reach and influence.

Second, the social and economic climate can drive changes in consumer behaviour, creating new opportunities for individuals to connect with their target audience. For instance, the increasing popularity of social media has made it easier for individuals to build relationships with potential customers and clients. Those who have effectively utilized social media platforms to build a strong personal brand can capitalize on this shift in consumer behaviour to further enhance their visibility and engagement.

Third, the social and economic climate can spark conversations and debates about important societal issues, providing individuals with a platform to share their perspectives and insights. For example, the ongoing debate about healthcare reform has created opportunities for individuals with expertise in the healthcare sector to share their knowledge and influence public discourse. By actively participating in these conversations, individuals can strengthen their personal brand and establish themselves as thought leaders in their field.

However, while the social and economic climate can create moments of momentum, it is also important to consider the issue of relevancy. Personal branding efforts must be aligned with the current trends and concerns of the target audience. Individuals who fail to adapt their messaging and strategies to the changing climate may find their efforts ineffective and irrelevant.

Strategies for Maintaining Relevance in Personal Branding

If I had not studied workforce engagement and kept up with the evolution of diversity, equity, and inclusion, no one would have called me to speak on the subject. It's vital, when it comes to putting your brand to action, to use your expertise and stay updated on current events and trends, to review different sources that are written through varied perspectives, and to network through attending relevant events.

Take the most up-to-date information you can find, examine what is happening, form your own opinion, and then share your perspective with your target audience. There are different ways to engage your audience, and a variety of platforms that you can choose from to use as focus points to communicate your personal brand.

As an example, I built my personal brand primarily on LinkedIn. While I could gain a following on other platforms, my target audience is executives, entrepreneurs, and event organizers. LinkedIn was an obvious choice. TikTok, on the other hand, seemed the least relevant platform for my messaging, despite its popularity.

Continuously refine your messaging in order to stay relevant over time. As your expertise grows and the social and economic climate evolves, ensure that your messaging remains relevant and up-to-date so you can avoid being a one-hit wonder. When you think about the song "Take On Me" by A-Ha from 1985, you think of 1985. While the song deserves credit for remaining a part of our lives so many years later, its legacy pales in contrast to that of Sting, who was not only creating great music back in 1985, but is still actively creating. A-Ha made a single catchy song, but as far as the public is concerned, that's all they are known for, and all their other music is ultimately irrelevant in this day and age.

The Relevance of an Embodied Personal Brand

Brand strategist Danielle Garber makes a case for embodying your brand by practicing what you preach. Garber notes, "Embodying your brand personality effectively creates a strong and memorable brand image. It goes beyond simply showcasing your products or services; it is about curating the conversation and expressing the authentic elements of your personality that align with your brand." Garber says, "Participating in activities and events that resonate with your brand's values and target audience can help you embody your brand's personality."

Showing up is active, not passive, and takes place when you reach out to connect. It takes place when you walk into a room of people who want to hear what you have to say, or when you press upload on that video post, even though you are scared.

Building a lasting brand also depends on knowing that hybrid points of engagement are crucial. During the tail end of 2017 and the front end of 2018, social media usage declined in the US and Canada for the first time since these statistics were recorded. The market had become too saturated. People logged out of Facebook, turned off their Twitter, and deleted their Snapchat apps with unanticipated regularity. Social media's exponential growth curve had reached its zenith. People started placing their valuable attention on other things, like taking a walk, talking directly to friends and family, or reading a book—activities that created connection.

To the chagrin of Silicon Valley, people rediscovered a real world beyond the laptop interface or the fancy smartphone touchscreen. Teens started choosing embodied connection over the virtual variety. Adult folks—many reading this book—deleted social media profiles and put down their iPads. Tech entrepreneurs panicked. "Have we lost?"

Then, after so many had deactivated their Facebook accounts, a comeback ensued. Around Christmas 2019, the mysterious plague from the East started stealthily advancing into the headline news. The Coronavirus was taking shape in the form of cruise ship guests plagued with fever and US airspace closed off to international travellers, followed soon by quarantines, school closures, and the frightening temporary extinction of toilet paper.

Seriousness and grief set in. People were confined to their homes and hospital beds as jobs and lives were lost in mass droves. Many people we knew and loved didn't make it. Compounding all the trouble, we couldn't connect with the people we love the most in an embodied way. Sure, we cloistered with neighbours or immediate family members, albeit from behind masks, but when we met through video meeting technology, the masks could come off. We could see the smiles on our colleagues' faces and, over time, we all realized that the digital connections during the pandemic are what sustained us.

Cut off from most physical connections, how did people respond? They downloaded the Facebook app they had deleted. They posted pictures. They messaged well wishes to all their friends. They let the people they cared about know that they were alive.

COVID, while we all wish we could abandon the conversation forever, provided us with a new, hybrid style of embodied leadership and the opportunity to learn from people of influence, no matter the obstacles. Influential leaders with personal brands and thought leadership platforms held meetings online and created educational courses and webinars accessible from anywhere. Once known for their presence and leadership on physical platforms, they have now transitioned to the digital realm, delivering immense value, often without any cost. Today, these same leaders integrate the power of being together in person with the broad reach of connectivity through technology. You too have a massive opportunity to show up on all mediums and contexts for greater brand bandwidth.

Embodying connection means showing up for your clients, customers, and team members in whatever venue is needed to make it work. It means meeting them on their turf from time to time, whether that's in a boardroom or a video conference room. It means learning some of the intricacies of their story so that you can build rapport and gain insight. With a bit of practice, you can transcend the challenge of the screen through the Three Acts of Engagement. My ideal way to show up is by sharing space and time with the other. But an introverted leader may show up more authentically in writing or through voiceover. Whatever the communication modality, embrace the fact that somebody, somewhere, needs to hear your message. Keeping this in mind will help you activate the courage you need to share yourself with the world.

I have given my signature keynote, "Unstoppable," on stage, and it also lives and breathes in digital form on YouTube and other sites. While I have a more substantial stage presence than a video presence, my story is built on the premise of walking the walk and helping others see that adversity can be their greatest strength.

I prefer to share my story in various ways that are reflective of how I best perform. The outlets I most often use are writing blogs and articles on LinkedIn, doing news media and podcast interviews, providing private coaching and mentoring, and, my favourite, speaking on stage. While living in a public fishbowl is unnecessary, your current and potential clients will seek some degree of access to your life and personal growth. You have agency regarding where you show up and what you choose to share. For example, I was in a pretty significant accident a while ago, requiring surgery and hospitalization. I shared my crash story with my audience on several platforms when I had recovered to the point where I was ready to write and talk about it. The experience directly related to what resilience in action looks like, a clear example that had nothing to do with garnering attention and everything to do with showing how I get through hard things so my audience is inspired to know that they can too. Being transparent and accessible with your audience reinforces the value you can create for them.

A Personal Brand in Action

Sting, now known as a multifaceted musician, has maintained his relevance throughout his illustrious career by consistently aligning his brand with causes he deeply cares about. He has leveraged his fame and influence to raise awareness and support for environmental conservation, social justice, and education. These efforts have not only reinforced his image as a thoughtful and engaged individual but have also connected him with a wider audience, extending his reach beyond the realm of music.

Sting's commitment to environmentalism dates back to the 1980s when he cofounded the Rainforest Fund with his wife, Trudie Styler. The organization works to protect rainforests and the indigenous communities that depend on them. Sting has been a tireless advocate for the rainforests, using his platform to educate the public about the importance of these vital ecosystems and the threats they face.

Beyond environmental concerns, Sting has also been a vocal advocate for social justice throughout his career. He has been a strong supporter of Amnesty International, performing at its benefit concerts and using his voice to speak out against human rights abuses around the world. He has also been involved in campaigns to end poverty and homelessness, and he has spoken out against war and violence.

Sting's active engagement in these causes has not only helped to raise awareness of important issues, but has also strengthened his brand identity. His association with these causes has made him more relatable and authentic to a wider audience, transcending his musical success and establishing him as a respected voice on social and environmental issues. This engagement has also helped to maintain his relevance over time, ensuring that he remains a prominent figure in the world of music and beyond.

Repeatedly I am asked what I attribute my success to. Above all else, my answer is action through unwavering work ethic and solid performance. I know long hours. I know hard work. I've held multiple concurrent jobs since I was eleven. I paid my own way through university and bought my first house at age 19. I've kept side hustles and lived on the road for significant stretches in my career. I could go on, but the reason I want to stress this is to make it clear that you do have to put skin in the game to build your career and your personal brand. If you see it as personal development, you will fall in love with the process like I have, and that love and your purpose will help you stay the course.

Four Great Questions

Aligning your actions can feel daunting. In the event you are not sure if what you are doing is geared to drive the outcomes you are looking for in effectively building your personal brand, I recommend four simple and powerful questions that you can use to decide what, in fact, you should do.

What is your expertise?

Be sure to focus on activating your strengths to your advantage.

What are you passionate about?

Remember that you are most engaged when you love what you do. Your audience engagement will be reflective of whether what you are doing is driven by passion.

What makes you different?

Always revert to communicating your UVP when it comes to acting on behalf of your brand.

What do you want to be known for?

Identify if the action you are considering taking is aligned with the impact you want to make now and the legacy you want to leave behind.

Networking with Strategic Intention

Making friends, putting yourself out there, attending events, and reaching out to people you want to connect with is absolutely crucial to the success of your personal brand. There's nothing slimy about networking when you ditch the sales speak and come from a place of authenticity.

Connections help to compound impact and legacy and make meaning of why you are sharing your personal brand in the first place. Introductions breed more introductions, clients, new opportunities, and referrals over time. Here's the thing though: be careful about saying yes to everyone and everything. Use the Four Great Questions as a guide for taking action in networking. Do the potential commitments align with what you want to have happen? If yes, create the space and go.

Putting your brand into action effectively depends on your ability to consistently identify what works, what doesn't work, what you learned, and what you will do differently. We have all gone to an event or committed to a meeting thinking that it made sense, only to leave knowing that it wasn't the best use of our time. Those instances will lessen as your UVP becomes more focused and understood, and the impact you are making unfolds. Navigating success involves a deep comprehension of your audience and where to find them. The journey to this understanding requires experimentation and, yes, you'll encounter some missteps along the way. However, these mistakes are valuable, offering insights that guide the trajectory of your progress.

CHAPTER 10:

MEASURING YOUR BRAND IMPACT

When you hold the reins of your brand's narrative, you are actively shaping its outcomes. These outcomes are a blend of how your audience perceives you, the feedback you receive, and both the positive and negative impacts that emerge. Good intentions are a start, but the actual results are the true measure of your brand's effectiveness. The results also reflect the consistency and authenticity with which you are cultivating your personal brand.

If your journey in building your personal brand is devoid of any criticism or challenges, it might be a sign that you're not pushing the boundaries enough. If some people don't like what you stand for, that means you *are* standing for something, and that can be a good sign, even if it is hard to digest at first. A part of personal brand building is being comfortable with not being for *everyone*. You will realize that it's far more important to concentrate on the key areas where you're gaining traction, and with the people who resonate with your personal brand. As you attract your target audience and refine your approach based on the strategies outlined in *Influence Unleashed*, the positive impacts of your efforts will amplify, likely becoming tenfold more significant than any negative feedback you receive.

Evaluating Audience Feedback

The first step in reviewing the results that come from your audience is identifying if, in fact, the audience you have is reflective of your target followership. What are the demographics of your target audience? Are you attracting them? Not all platforms supply you with specific metrics, so in cases where you cannot see the details that relate to various demographic indicators, you can still gauge who is showing up through the communication you are receiving.

The audience that is attracted to your brand as you use the Influence Unleashed method will become very clear. As you learn who is showing up, you will be able to discern how, in the eyes of others, you are putting yourself out there. This feedback can help you sharpen your messaging, learn what it really feels like to "be yourself," and consider that the long game is in the evolution of your personal brand.

When I was formally acknowledged as one of only 30 "Out Executives" worldwide several years ago during my time at IBM, I had been fairly open about my sexuality and that I had been married to a woman. Little did I realize how important it was for others to see more diverse faces coming forward. In my case, at the time, I was the only open queer/bisexual executive amongst the 30; all of the others identified as gay men or lesbian women. My standing up reinforced the integrity of my story, my authenticity, and brand identity. A deeper layer of myself was exposed and I became increasingly passionate as a member of the LGBTQ+ community. Some of my colleagues lived in parts of the world where their sexuality would not be as readily accepted as it is in North America.

I loved standing for them by standing up as myself. While I could not see exact metrics, I received a great many emails, Slack messages, and phone calls from my target audience that told me that my messaging was aligned with what they wanted and needed to hear.

Understanding the hopes and dreams of your audience has probably laid the groundwork for who will seek out your distinct value proposition. As a speaker on DEI and women's advocacy, I am often contacted by leaders who are not in the minority to help them improve their systems, processes, and human resources departments. They see what I stand for, understand that I have facts and experience to back up everything I do, and they respect me for it enough to know that they can ask me to come in and help. My audience is diverse because my platform encourages diversity. This has included those who I don't directly advocate for but want to advocate with me.

The feedback data you receive will help you identify the extent to which your UVP is, in fact, solving the pain points and challenges of your audience. Scrutinize that data carefully; use it to help refine and improve your personal brand. It's vital to review the content of your message, including the topics on which you speak, the content type, keywords, and the platforms or mediums you are using.

What does this look like for those of us engaged in the important work of building and sustaining a strong personal brand? In a nutshell, we need to be comfortable digging into the data. What does the profile of my followership look like? What do the audience engagement results say about my leadership? Are my social media metrics growing or declining?

How often are my posts and long-form pieces shared on social media? What's the traffic look like on my personal website? Are my online followers growing? Am I getting more asks for presentations and interviews?

Have you ever Googled yourself? Try it. Write down the top four results that come up. When I do this, the top four search results are, in order, my website and then my LinkedIn, Instagram, and X (previously known as Twitter) profiles. So Google yourself, and then reflect on the text that shows up with this search. What would your audience learn about you if they Google you? In my case they would learn in the first 30 seconds of reading that I am a keynote speaker, published author, dynamic executive, and a tireless advocate for equity, social justice, Whole Human Leadership, and positive workplace culture. You will also see many links to articles, media appearances, and podcasts coming up through the search pages. This is an example of one's personal brand results at a glance—and it is powerful.

Every one of the platforms you are on provides you the opportunity to optimize your profile. I highly recommend you list the top platforms that are core to your personal brand and do an audit, starting with your profile picture. I didn't mention that when you Google my name, my profile picture appears in a thumbnail to the right of the search results. When I click on Google Images, all of the profile pictures I have used for the articles and appearances I have done populate in the search. Does your profile picture reflect your personal brand? In mine, I often stand in a power pose reflective of my core values of radical candor and no excuses. The way we are seen matters, and you have control over it.

Make sure your picture and every word that is written about you are consistent across all your profiles. Develop and deploy a list of brand-defining keywords that relate to what you want to be known for and appeal to the audience you want to attract. In auditing your platform, search for inconsistencies and outdated or off-brand messaging. Get rid of it if you find it, and replace it with your personal brand keywords.

Brand Evaluation Tools

Measuring the strength and impact of your personal brand can be challenging because it often involves qualitative as well as quantitative factors. However, there are several methods and metrics you can use to assess and monitor your personal brand's effectiveness:

- **Feedback and Perceptions**: Gather feedback from peers, clients, mentors, and others from your network. Understand how they perceive you and your brand. This can provide valuable insights into your brand's impact and areas for improvement.

- **Social Media Engagement**: Monitor your engagement metrics on social media platforms. Likes, shares, comments, and followers can indicate the reach and resonance of your brand. Pay attention to the quality of interactions as well, such as meaningful conversations or connections made. On LinkedIn, you can capture their own assessment of the strength of your brand and overall engagement with your network by viewing what they refer to as your Social Selling Index.

- **Professional Opportunities**: Track the professional opportunities that arise as a result of your personal brand. These could include job offers, speaking engagements, consulting requests, or collaborations. An increase in such opportunities often signals a strong and impactful brand.

- **Content Reach and Influence**: If you produce content (blogs, articles, videos, podcasts, etc.), measure its reach and influence. Look at views, shares, citations, and the extent to which your content is referenced or used by others.

- **Network Growth and Quality**: Evaluate the growth and quality of your professional network. A growing network that includes influential and relevant contacts can be a sign of an effective personal brand.

- **Career Progression**: Assess how your personal brand has influenced your career trajectory. Consider promotions, recognitions, or achievements that can be attributed, at least in part, to your personal branding efforts.

- **Mentoring and Impact on Others**: Reflect on your role as a mentor or influencer. The ability to positively inspire, guide, or impact others' careers or lives can be a strong indicator of the strength of your personal brand.

- **Goal Alignment**: Check how well your personal branding aligns with and supports your long-term goals. If your brand is helping you move toward these goals, it's a sign of its effectiveness.

- **Online Presence and Reputation**: Analyze your online presence and reputation. Tools like Google Alerts and various social media monitoring tools can help track how often you're mentioned online and the context of these mentions.

- **Personal Satisfaction and Fulfillment**: Finally, consider your personal satisfaction and fulfilment. If your personal brand accurately reflects who you are and is aligned with your values, and if you feel fulfilled by your professional life, these are strong indicators of a successful personal brand.

Remember, personal branding is not just about external validation, but also about internal consistency and alignment with your values, goals, and vision. Regular evaluation and adjustment are key to maintaining a strong and impactful presence.

Brené Brown, at one point in her life, considered herself as a researcher, an introvert who never imagined having the audience she has today. Gary Vaynerchuk set out on a mission to grow his family's business, not knowing that he would garner attention and success through simply being his boisterous, chatty self. Andrew Huberman wisely accepted the recommendation that he start a podcast, but with little belief that it would be anything other than a fun experiment. Ruth Bader Ginsburg surely never could have projected that she would inspire future generations of women clamoring for coffee mugs or T-shirts, like the one I have in my drawer that says, "Where there are nine."

I have no doubt that your voice, when projected through the Influence Unleashed methodology, will make a difference in at least one person's life. But my goal for you is bigger than that. I want to en*courage* you to own who you are, and in the process, spread the contagion of personal branding as a form of agency that will help the world become a better, more diverse and equitable place to live. And if that's not your goal, maybe you can at least be like Bessie the Coburg Dairy Cow and make predicting the weather a little easier and more fun. ·

SUMMARY

The Influence Unleashed method is a guiding framework to building and managing your personal brand for professional advancement. It emphasizes that personal branding is not just about self-promotion. It's about creating a meaningful and lasting impact. You can be an extrovert, introvert, or somewhere in-between, but you must be courageous, vulnerable, and authentic. How others experience you will be reflective of the persona you create. Strive to be one who is humble and accessible while simultaneously clear on who you are, what you do, and what you stand for. Now that you have gone through the framework, I hope you are thinking about the lived experiences that you want to share. And I hope you are working on building the cornerstone that differentiates personal branding from expertise: establishing trust.

When you began moving through the Influence Unleashed methodology, you had goals or outcomes in mind. Whether specific or vague, you began with ideas of what you want to have happen as a result of putting in the effort to build your personal brand. Reaching this point of the book, I hope that those goals have been clarified, and that you now feel empowered to achieve them. I also hope that you remain curious, and that you are confident that having agency over the public expression of what you do and who you are will ultimately provide fulfillment, opening doors that align with your passion, interests, and core values.

Metaphors for Remembering What Brings Your Personal Brand to Life

Like solar power is to the windmill or electricity is to an environmentally friendly vehicle, there are natural resources that you have tapped into throughout this book. These natural forces create the energy that is critical for your personal brand to come alive in a way that fully unleashes your influence. The *Why* of your brand is driven by internal emotional mechanics, the Three Acts of Engagement, that lead to uncovering your passion, interests, core values, and lived experiences you want to share. All essential elements necessary to define your UVP.

Your UVP is like the wind, the external driving force that carries your messaging across platforms, auditoriums, and boardrooms. Think of the value Bessie the Coburg Cow created, literally with the wind, as a figurative construct to inspire you to visualize the unforeseen possibilities that come from creating value from your point of distinction. When people feel the value of your offering, they come to you. It's contagious. As the contagion spreads and the value is realized, the scope of your impact becomes more apparent. You realize what's possible on a larger scale (or more meaningful scale, if you want a small, select, curated audience). An audience that is driven by your *Why* and reaping the benefits of your UVP creates a lasting impression: the legacy of your personal brand. Consistent action, evaluation, and learning ensue, as does the satisfying confirmation that you understand that this is your life's work.

Influence Unleashed Requires You to Be You

From becoming a keynote speaker to being a sought-after consultant, the things that you want to have happen are possible when you reach for everything the Influence Unleashed methodology offers. You can do this if you are an introvert like Andrew Huberman or an extrovert like Gary Vaynerchuk. Think about the arena of your influence and how, if there were no obstacles, you would unleash all of that value you wish to share with people. Your core audience can extend to the nosebleed seats like Sting's or remain a select, influential few like Warren Buffet's.

Embracing the Influence Unleashed method is about bringing the essence of your true self to the forefront. We've delved deep into the art of brand building, exploring a plethora of impactful words. Now, it's time for you to personify them. From your thoughts to your actions, from your internal beliefs to your outward expression, you become a living, breathing symbol of your personal brand in every aspect of your life. It's about "walking the talk," staying true to your core values, and being propelled by your *Why*. These are the dynamic forces at the heart of unleashing your influence. Remember, it's the tangible outcomes, the results you create and the connections you make, that truly count. Regularly ask yourself, is the full version of you showing up? Commit to representing your brand faithfully and applying the principles of the Three Acts of Engagement, both internally and externally.

Courage. Maybe you feel it in your heart, maybe you feel it all over your body. Perhaps your heart races a little bit, and in spite of doubts or fears you are showing up to do what it takes to make what you want happen. Using courage is mandatory for reaching higher states of emotion like bliss and joy. Go for it! I implore you.

Vulnerability. It's okay if your hands tremble, tears brim in your eyes, or your throat feels dry. These are natural responses when you're sharing from a place of genuine openness and rawness, a space that demands courage to access. This vulnerability is about recognizing that your experiences, feelings, and thoughts could be exactly what someone else needs to hear. It's about connecting others with their own stories, inspiring them through the authenticity of your personal brand. Embrace this moment, speak your truth, and discover the transformative impact of open sharing. And remember, it's equally important to respect your own privacy and set clear boundaries.

Authenticity. It's time to celebrate! The days of pretending to be someone else to gain followers or network connections are over. Embracing your true self might seem daunting, but remember, your courage is there to support you. When you're authentic, there's a sense of liberation. You'll find yourself more relaxed, engaging with others effortlessly and confidently, knowing that your real charm is what draws people in. This could manifest in your unique sense of humour on stage or in your creatively expressive attire. It's the voice that your friends know and adore. When we act authentically, there's no room for regret. It's a deeply compassionate act, generously enriching those who experience it.

Throughout *Influence Unleashed*, so many powerful words and ideas were introduced and examined. From identity to legacy, if all of them live and breathe with you in every boardroom, stage, interview, YouTube Video, and LinkedIn post, building your personal brand will be the highlight of your life. We have witnessed this with every single powerful human who has been presented in this book. Remember that unhealthy comparison steals joy, but being inspired by others is a motivator that you can do it too. Get inspired. Watch the magic of people who are doing it and find yours too.

"People do business with people they like and trust and, therefore, *want* to do business with." Thank you for trusting me to be your guide on your personal branding journey. If you are still struggling with the belief that what you have to offer is important, I send you the courage to step into the arena anyway and watch that belief system crumble as you start to align with your core values. Courage. Vulnerability. Authenticity. Repeat.

My Gift to You Going Forward

I hope that by reading about the powerful impact the people who have influenced me have had on the world, you can understand the scope of transformation that comes from just one person stepping up to the plate. Whether you feel doubtful or confident that you have a UVP, whether you can't wait or feel apprehensive to forge your pathway forward, I strongly recommend working it out on paper with strategic intentionality. With that recommendation, I offer you a special gift I've crafted: a companion workbook filled with brand analysis and strategy resources, thoughtfully designed to complement the lessons you've absorbed from this book. You can find this on my website: www.victoria-pelletier.com.

Now that you've delved into the pages of *Influence Unleashed* and absorbed the wisdom within, it's official! You're prepared to embark on a journey of self-discovery and transformation like no other. You're primed to make bold, authentic moves that will define your path to success. Congratulations! Now go out and make your mark on the world!

ACKNOWLEDGEMENTS

In the process of crafting this book on personal branding, I've deeply reflected on the multitude of influences and support systems that have shaped my narrative and professional identity. This journey has been less about finding pre-established paths and more about carving out my own, learning from a diverse array of experiences and individuals.

I extend heartfelt thanks to the unknowing mentors in my personal and professional sphere. While our paths in branding may have differed, your insights and feedback have been invaluable in shaping my perspectives. Each interaction, whether brief or extended, has contributed a piece to the mosaic of my personal brand. I also want to extend gratitude to the acclaimed thought leaders I've quietly observed and learned from.

To my partner, Dany, your unwavering support and belief in my vision have been the bedrock of my endeavours. Your encouragement and the shared joy in each milestone have made this journey all the more fulfilling. You continue to be my greatest cheerleader and confidant.

I must also thank my dear friend, Jen, who has been a sounding board and a source of relentless encouragement. Your knack for seeing through the noise and helping me focus on what truly matters has been a guiding light.

To my children, Zoë and Jordyn, you are the very heart of my world. Witnessing your growth and navigating life with its myriad of challenges and triumphs has been a constant source of inspiration. Your perspectives have enriched my understanding of personal branding in today's dynamic world.

Lastly, to my readers and followers who have engaged with my work and shared their stories—your experiences and feedback have not only enriched this book, but also continually shape my approach to personal branding.

This book is a testament to all of you who have been part of my journey. Thank you for your part in my story, for the wisdom shared, and the lessons learned. I look forward to our continuing to evolve and grow together.

ABOUT THE AUTHOR

Victoria Pelletier is a seasoned corporate executive with over two decades of leadership experience, including roles as COO, President, and CEO. Her career has been marked by a passion for inspiring positive change and growth in organizations, a journey also defined by her commitment to continuous personal learning, growth, and resilience.

Victoria's contributions have earned her numerous awards and recognition for her dedication and advocacy of diversity, equity, and inclusion, as well as for her significant history of mentorship in the workplace.

She is a sought after media guest and professional keynote speaker. Victoria regularly shares her insights on topics such as Whole Human Leadership, developing resilience, and personal branding, while always striving to inspire and empower others on their journeys.

Victoria's other books include *Unstoppable: Changemakers Who Dare to Make a Difference* and the soon-to-be released *The Power of Whole Human Leadership: Managing Modern Workers Toward Purpose and Profit.* You may follow or connect with Victoria via her website: www.victoria-pelletier.com